MAN AND UNIVERSE

CHRONICLE

OF A CHRISTIAN-HERMETIC SCHOOL

Compiled by Work Group 'Atanor'

Serebrov Boeken Publishing

ISBN13: 9789083267647; 978-90-832676-4-7
© Serebrov Boeken, The Hague, 2022
Pubisher: Guram Kochi
Telefoon: +31 70 352 15 65
E-mail: info@serebrovboeken.nl
Website: www.serebrovboeken.nl

English translation of the Russian book 'Учение Мастера Джи, часть III'
Editor: Gouri Gozalov c.s.
Translator: Gouri Gozalov

Design: Maria Toonen en Gouri Gozalov
The Book of Psalms: http://www.sacredbible.org/catholic/OT-21_Psalms.htm
The Four Gospels: http://www.sacredbible.org/catholic/NT-00_Gospels.htm

The content of this book has been compiled by Work Group 'Atanor' with the use of the transcriptions of conversations between Vladimir Stepanov (Master G), head of a Christian-Hermetic School (aka Ship 'Argo', aka Ship of Fools, aka Slippery Deck), and his disciple Konstantin Serebrov.

All rights reserved. No part of this publication may be reproduced or transmitted in any form or by any means, electronic or mechanical, including photocopy and recording, or stored in a retrieval system, without the written permission of the publisher.

Vladimir Stepanov (Master G) with his disciples, 2005

TABLE OF CONTENTS

Chapter 1. How to let a spiritual idea inspire you
and then implement it in your life?
On the importance of the influence of the third force 12

Chapter 2. Each civilization brings with it
a new initiatory wind.
How to learn how to work in a team 14

Chapter 3. About the Arsenal ensemble.
A few words about the Master.
How to learn to love your neighbours 17

Chapter 4. The most important thing in the School
is to establish a sincere and heartful contact
between disciples. About the sense of style 19

Chapter 5. What does it mean
to be a man of the Path? About Mount Kaph
and the bird Simurg 21

Chapter 6. The search for a spiritual Master.
The task of the wandering of the Master
and his disciples in the outside world.
A new etheric initiation. The parable
of the invisibly growing seed 24

Chapter 7. Conscious suffering
or how to deal with inner temperature 26

Chapter 8. How to burn the infernal traits
and cultivate noble ones. About initiatory literature.
About the sensitivity of the heart.
The subtle atmosphere in the School
helps the disciples to grow 28

Chapter 9. It is necessary to consider the influence
of the external environment. On the importance
of spiritual practices and stalking.
Vertical creativity on the Ship of Fools 31

Chapter 10. How to come in contact
with the collective soul of all Adamites?
Who is Kulturträger? About the elevated
essential relationships in the worlds of light 34

Chapter 11. Architecture that balances
heaven and earth. Freemasonry.
How to become the one who follows the Path 36

Chapter 12. The era of rudeness and lack of culture.
About the culture of everyday life 40

Chapter 13. Cultivation of subtle perception.
Hermetic mind. The fusion of Hermetic
and Christian currents. Creative experiment
of the new chivalry 42

Chapter 14. About Fairy and G.
White and black initiations. On the hermetic initiation.
Hermetic knowledge is protected. How to avoid
switching to the dark current 45

Chapter 15. About how to properly train the disciples
of the Ship. About one's work on oneself 48

Chapter 16. How to pass the test by the powers
of chaos? 52

Chapter 17. The refined atmosphere
of the alchemical Ray. What does 'communication
on the energy of the belly' mean?
How to develop subtle perception 53

Chapter 18. Adultery is a crime. How to curb your instincts? Working with the ladies on the Argonauts' Ship 56

Chapter 19. About deep work on oneself and the benefits of physical labour. On the importance of mastering various professions... 59

Chapter 20. About conflicts and points of tension. About passionarity and overcoming obstacles on the Path of salvation 62

Chapter 21. About the struggle between the higher and lower vehicles of human monad. About the inner battle.. 64

Chapter 22. About the alchemical crucible of the soul and about alchemical melting. On the work of the Ship of the Argonauts in the sephira Malkuth 65

Chapter 23. On the problems of magnetization and demagnetization. About conscious work on yourself. On the highest Sephirah of the Tree of Sephirot................ 67

Chapter 24. About subtlety and coarseness of the soul. About the styles of behaviour 70

Chapter 25. About the alchemical songs of Admiral. About the fallacious philosophy of Panicovsky................... 72

Chapter 26. How to get rid of loutish behaviour and reach the essential level of communication? How to cultivate courage 75

Chapter 27. About Master G. When the soul is shrouded in darkness. Do not postpone the performing of spiritual practices until tomorrow. How to cultivate willpower........................ 77

Chapter 28. About the mission of the Lord
Jesus Christ. About the Universal proclamation
brought by G.. 80

Chapter 29. About subtlety and coarseness.
How to unite the two Traditions, the Hermetic
and the Christian ones 82

Chapter 30. About character building. How to obtain
the subtle perception of the world. It is important
to immerse in the depths of your Spirit every day.
On the need to build a path of ascending.
Separation of the subtle from the coarse............................. 85

Chapter 31. How not to waste the current incarnation?
On the need for essential communication 89

Chapter 32. About how important it is to love your
neighbours. About a cold attitude towards people.
What does 'to love' mean? It is important to warm
your heart... 91

Chapter 33. Prayers to the Lord.. 93

Chapter 34. On the sin of adultery and how to
transform karma 94

Chapter 35. In order to reach the higher worlds
of the Heavenly Father, the disciple has to undergo
the alchemical transformation of his soul............................ 97

Chapter 36. Why is there more demand from older
disciples? About G's spiritual guidance
and an open heart.. 100

Chapter 37. How to warm a frozen heart?
Keeping your heart clean is important
for resisting the powers of evil 103

Chapter 38. About the rules of the spiritual schools.
How to create Botticelli's Spring instead of a gloomy
and dreary atmosphere?.. 105

Chapter 39. About alchemical situations
and work with different 'selves' 108

Chapter 40. About the purpose of human
incarnation. About alchemical transformation.
Heavy karma interferes with following
the Path of Enlightenment 110

Chapter 41. On the subtle atmosphere,
essential communication and the benefits of prayer ... 112

Chapter 42. How not to become demagnetized
in a new place. How to behave on the front line.
How to become an experienced helmsman 115

Chapter 43. A person's inner spiritual world
is his true treasure. About the fragility of the world.
About the two main commandments of Jesus Christ ... 117

Chapter 44. Morning is a great time to immerse
yourself in the silence of your heart. About the inner
world of Lord Henry. On the importance of essential
communication. About freedom. On self-observation
and one's sincerity in relation to oneself 119

Chapter 45. Life is like a refined chess game.
How to strengthen Arjuna's Working Group.
A pure soul is a young girl. How to get rid of
gloominess. On the benefits of a diary of inner states. 122

Chapter 46. How to obtain subtlety of perception?
Repentance frees the disciple from his karmic burden 125

Chapter 47. How to enter the magic space of chess.
About the Albedo stage 127

Chapter 48. About the four Card Kingdoms 129

Chapter 49. On how to transform one's horizontal
being into a ritual, dedicated to God. It is important
not to lose feedback with each other. How to withstand
the Heavenly Fire. What is the right way to partake
of the Gospel 132

Chapter 50. Comments on the film 'Cyrano' 134

Chapter 51. About the struggle for 'a place in the sun'.
On inspiration in art. 'There are no delays
to visit God.' How to stop playing the role
of the cheap opera singer Giglio Fava................................... 137

Chapter 52. About the main problems arising
in the creation of a close-knit team on the Ship.
What is needed for establishing feedback between
the Argonauts. How to link to the Hermetic Tradition 140

Chapter 53. On the importance of astral travel.
About establishing contact with higher humanity. How
the knowledge of the stellar tradition came to Earth . 143

Chapter 54. About four aspects of the stellar
knowledge. The disciple must be honest with
himself. About the Sufi tradition. Can common
people accept the Hermetic tradition? 145

Chapter 55. The theme of the VIIth Arcanum:
opposition of the black and white sphinxes.
The theme of the XVth Arcanum: how to overcome
Baphomet in yourself? Our goal is to learn how
to control both sphinxes 147

Chapter 56. About conscious and mechanical suffering. How to rebuild your life in a vertical way? About the purposeful blow of George the Victorious to the dragon 150

Chapter 57. About the defence of one's pride by means of a duel. How to become a knight of the spirit and curb the dragon? On the principles of the Old and New Testaments. About sore points and how to work them out.. 152

Chapter 58. About the highest honour and the experiences of the divine soul. It is important to find time for spiritual development. The Ship of Argonauts helps disciples to realize their cosmic soul. What does honesty with yourself mean 154

Chapter 59. About stalking and hermeticism 155

Chapter 60. The goal of spiritual wanderers is to restore the link to the Creator of the Universe. About the Hermetic Tradition. About Sufism. Universal wisdom and higher humanity............................ 158

Chapter 61. About the Path of Ascent which is built on the mystical Ship. To contact the cosmic Tradition, you need to go through an alchemical transformation 160

Chapter 62. About the necessary conditions for the alchemical reaction. What does 'being placed in the alchemical crucible' mean.. 162

Chapter 63. How can you tell a real Master from a fake one? About the need to search for the Master. About the three types of influence: A, B and C. About the influence of the Sun and the Moon 164

Chapter 64. About different levels of existence in the Universe. The vertical and horizontal scale of human values. About the earthly soul, the universal soul and the Higher Self. What does it mean to love a person 166

Chapter 65. Formation of the magnetic centre: spiritual quest. In Search of the alchemical School and the Master. Harmonization of the magnetic centre 168

Chapter 66. On how a disciple can convey the current of light. What happens to a disciple who has fallen under the influence of dark forces. How to get out of negative states. It is important to understand what state you are in 170

Chapter 67. Having become crystallized, we act mechanically. Discussion on building the School space 173

Chapter 68. About the spiritual patronage of St. Nicholas the Wonderworker and the holy apostles John the Theologian, Peter and Andrew the First-Called. About Martha and Mary 176

Chapter 69. The School helps disciples to immerse in themselves. About the relationship between the Master and the disciple. About three types of disciples in the fairy tales 179

Supplement: Practices of purification and awakening 202

Chapter 1. How to let a spiritual idea inspire you and then implement it in your life? On the importance of the influence of the third force

6th April 1986 Tashkent, People's Palace

Each spiritual idea carried by the etheric tradition has its own mystical wind, its unique atmosphere and energy. In alchemical terms, every spiritual idea of the etheric initiation is saturated with specific alchemical metals and metaphysical substances. If the disciple assimilates a spiritual idea that the Master shares with him and becomes inspired by it in his heart, soul and spirit, he alchemically reacts with it and thus his alchemical composition changes. The disciple absorbs those alchemical metals, those metaphysical substances that this idea brings from the higher worlds.

If the disciple manages to fully realize this idea, it will change his inner composition to such an extent that he will begin to communicate with the inhabitants of the higher worlds.

If the disciple manages to completely surrender to Christ, to become imbued with His commandments to the depths of all his "selves", these are his contradictory subpersonalities, then he will be able to gradually transform his inner ore into gold, he will be able to become a Christian.

A true Christian is he who follows the commandments of Jesus Christ and is the bearer of His impulse. He, who attracts the currents of Jesus into his heart and melts the ore of his soul in the alchemical fire. He, who sacrifices his efforts for the sake of raising the fallen universe. But for this, the disciple needs to have a high level of spiritual being and will- power, which is capable of resisting the numerous temptations of life.

In order to realize ideas on the level of being, the disciple needs to make daily efforts in working on himself. This means to undergo the purification stage and perform the practices of awakening that transform our inner lead into spiritual gold.

Following the hoopoe, climb the holy mountain Kaph, to the mystical bird Simurg. There are behind the spiritual ideas which the Master shares with the disciple the higher spiritual beings, who are part of the Ray that conveys the aid from the higher worlds and the impulse of love of the Creator of the Universe. By integrating spiritual ideas into his life, the disciple purifies, transforms and strengthens his initially raw soul. If he goes through all the stages of alchemical transformation in the right way, then he has the opportunity to come in contact with the Source of eternal bliss, that is with our Lord.

Chapter 2. Each civilization brings with it a new initiatory wind. How to learn how to work in a team

Now is the time to talk about what is new in each emerging civilization. The initiatory moment of each civilization carries within itself the space of new spiritual ideas, built on new alchemical metals, on new precious substances, carries its own special and unique, mystical wind. China, India, Sumer, Assyria, Babylon, Ancient Egypt, Greece, Sparta, Rome, Byzantium, Catholic Europe, Orthodox Russia - they all carry their spiritual initiatory winds, filled with completely different mystical ideas, a mysterious and unique atmosphere.

We must learn to recognize the spiritual winds of ancient civilizations and to investigate them. It is necessary to enter their mystical atmosphere, to let our soul get in touch with their spiritual traditions. And only then can a fully-fledged ideological and alchemical fusion occur within us.

To enter the atmosphere of each civilization, one must possess a high level of spiritual being. And such a being is built up not only by years of studying various cultures and ancient civilizations, but by having spent some incarnations in those civilizations.

At School we learn to work as a cohesive whole. Disciples with different interests, abilities, who have one task - to climb Mount Kaf staying in resonance with the Ray of the School as a single team. Disciples need to learn to take into account each other's interests, while fulfilling the task. Stop behaving like a circular firing squad, stop doing this little waltz and start considering the interests of others. Otherwise, we will destroy the team effort and split its power into many single efforts. And this weakens the influence of the School's Ray on the materialistic environment of the city by hundreds or even thousands of times.

I see a slight mistrust in your eyes, but this is easy to prove with the example of our small jazz band of 11 people. Each of them is doing his own thing and is completely different from the others. Being on his own each of us can do very little, but having united in one team, we travel all over the Soviet Union and work miracles. Together, we bring the good news to all cities through popular jazz music, change the atmosphere of cities, and fill it with the influence of the School's Ray that carries etheric initiation. But alone none of us is able to do this. The team of the jazz band consists of six musicians: a saxophonist, who is also the leader of the band, a solo guitarist, bass guitarist, drummer, percussionist, pianist and manager of the band. And also the School Triangle, which does all the maintenance work. This is an excellent example of the teamwork of a group of people of completely different interests, temperaments and specialties, which allows the band to move around the country without any obstacles. And this is where the whole secret of a successful team influence on the broad masses of people is hidden.

But in our School circle there is still no team spirit, you all constantly quarrel with each other. I repeat to you once again: I need you all together, not each separately.

Each disciple is unique and can therefore make a unique contribution to the common cause. Remember, 'School' means few disciples, but many beads, precious spaces, and teaching situations.

Remember the fairy tale about Bubble, who recruited various specialists to his team - a non-stop drinker, a glutton, a runner and many others. And so, having gathered such a peculiar team, he went on a mission. And when, in the course of fulfilling his mission, various insurmountable obstacles arose, there was always a professional in his team to solve one or other particular problem hands-down.

To learn how to overcome the barrier of alienation between each and all of you, you need to start studying the ideas of stage-manager Stanislavsky. The spirit of his ideas will help you understand how to resolve easily almost all problems and disagreements between you. And outside this spirit it is difficult to find what are the ties between different disciples and how to allow each individual to exist on an equal footing with the others. A theatrical group is, in fact, a close-knit team, where all feel each other and at the right time can give a helping hand. A team is called close-knit if all its members can play and improvise with each other without any offense or condemnation. For Stanislavsky always talked about group work in an actor's team. When all members of the team trust each other, the play runs spontaneously and with inspiration.

We must consciously get used to all the unpleasant manifestations of our neighbours. For this to happen in reality, and not only in words, you need to reconsider your negative reactions and say regularly prayers of forgiveness. When you will curb your dark twin, you can learn to work as a team. And in the future, you will bring the good news of Enlightenment to the farthest corners of the universe in order to lend a helping hand to souls seeking salvation. Then, and in the yet to come incarnations, we will meet again to continue the School work.

Chapter 3. About the Arsenal ensemble. A few words about the Master. How to learn to love your neighbours

18th April1987 Tashkent, Palace of Culture

Kasyan: 'With the help of the Arsenal ensemble, we are gradually preparing our country for the third millennium. For this a close-knit group of musicians is required, which is on friendly terms with the Triangle, that is Master G and his two disciples, Kasyan and Gouri, and allows the G's metaphysical impulses to influence their creativity. Thus the Ray, through the mystical atmosphere of music, rolls its etheric wave to people.

G remains an absolutely mysterious person unknown to us. More often than not, we see him kind and gentle. He, like a caring Papa Gepetto, will dry tears and put wise of anything at all to wooden Pinocchio, that is his disciples. But when in order to melt the instinctive centre, G turns from a good teacher into a benefactor, it is impossible to even approach him. He needs to do so because the Ouroboros does not understand gentle remarks, only a blow of the spear of George the Victorious can pacify it. If G does not play the role of a caring Teacher, then the distance between him and us is enormous. Love for the Lord burns in his heart, and ours are drawn to the warmth of the soul.

G constantly teaches us the art of loving one's neighbour. This is an incredibly difficult science that must be comprehended throughout our lives. G set a task for me, to build a Path along which human souls could climb to the Creator of the Universe. In this way I can unfold my vertical creativity at School.

The Master teaches us how to create a heartfelt atmosphere around us. But in order to assimilate this knowledge, the disciple must purify his soul and warm his heart.

Passions alienate us from the Lord, block the path to salvation. The holy fathers say that a person himself is not able to conquer them, therefore one must ask the Lord for help.
1. Pride can be defeated by love for the Creator of the Universe and for one's neighbours.
2. Despondency by prayer and gratitude to God;
3. Vanity by humility;
4. Anger by meekness, patience and mercy towards people;
5. Gluttony by moderation and fasting;
6. Fornication by modesty and chastity.
Then the essence will feel love for the Lord.

Chapter 4. The most important thing in the School is to establish a sincere and heartful contact between disciples. About the sense of style

19th April 1987 Frunze, teahouse

As soon as the disciples managed to establish in the School a sincere and heartful contact with each other at the level of all their centres, then the situation is experiencing the moment of the heyday of Botticelli's spring. As soon as the sincere contact is lost, then immediately everyone becomes bored and uninterested.

It is here that the art of kaif-master is required. It teaches how to organize the space in which sincere and heartful contact can take place. This, again, is a whole science of life, a special level of being necessary to be a kaif-master. You need to learn to warm the students with the warmth of your heart, establish a contact on the level of essence, please them, take care, unobtrusively find out what they need.

When you have managed to establish essential contact with your neighbours, it is as if beautiful flowers bloom in your soul. And we feel love for the Creator of the Universe, for people, and we can also catch the impulse of beauty and creativity emanating from the higher worlds of the Heavenly Father.

Master G to Kasyan: "If contact is achieved between you and me at the level of the soul, and you are the tip of the spear of Archangel Michael, then you can rotate your cogwheel and set in motion the cogwheels of those disciples who are connected with you in their soul and their heart.

If you are in resonance with the mystical wind of the Ray, burn with its spiritual ideas and perform the practices of awakening, you can inspire other students to do this.

In this way, the whole country can be gradually changed.

When energy will be given to save all of humanity, then our Triangle-alloy should not disintegrate. You can intensify your heart-to-heart contact with disciples and statues of the School, and they will all be pleased.

The most important thing in the School is the sincere and heartfelt contact between its disciples, which is the basis of all relationships in the School. Now we need to focus our efforts on strengthening contact with local 'hares' and with Arsenal. For they are the unconscious apostles. In Sufism this situation is called "Gulistan Garden".

Our task is to become an all-human. To get in touch with a team of people, you need to try to meet up all the requirements of each member of that team to you. If you accept their claims sincerely and cordially, then any tense atmosphere will quickly be dissolved. You must accept all the demands, no matter how absurd they may seem to you, and try to function in a situation where everyone is right except yourself. And instead of transforming others, transform yourself. This also is not an easy job, but this is the only way out. Our main problem is selfishness: for some reason it seems to us that we behave impeccably, and everyone else is wrong.

Selfishness can be conquered by humility. Find the strength to take the other person's point of view and admit that you were wrong.

Style is a person. The disciple must develop a sense of style. Each era has its own style of expression. People communicate with each other through gesture, facial expressions, words, through the atmosphere, with eyes, with a call of the heart, deed, action. A certain wave emanating from the soul and heart of a person is called a personal wind. A refined, educated person can convey the atmosphere of different eras and cultures. We still need to learn how to create an atmosphere of love, warmth and cordiality in various situations.

Chapter 5. What does it mean to be a man of the Path? About Mount Kaph and the bird Simurg

24th April 1987, Frunze

We are the tip of the spear of the Archangel Michael, and this spear goes into the stars. And we are the "Triangle", also Fairy and Admiral. Everything becomes sacralised through our presence, you have seen the evidence of this. Because behind us there is a huge universal spiritual School, a continent, a huge help and power of the highest humanity. It was given to us for organizing an alchemical School, for creating a fusion of Christian and Hermetic impulses on Earth.

And you always have a choice. If you weaken inside yourself and indulge in self-interest, get bogged down in the routine of horizontal life, stop transforming your earthly nature into a spiritual one, you will immediately fall into a sludge. That is, you will lose the connection with your higher 'Self', you will lose the connection with the Lord, with the Ray of the School. But if you will hold out, you will be like disciples strolling down an alley of statues. Then you will be able to be a man of the Path - this is an inner state in which you are connected with your higher consciousness, with the Creator of the Universe, and love for all people flows from your heart.

As soon as you abandon this spiritualized state, you become a statue. You can practice magic, open schools, but this will be your private creativity, not connected with the creativity of the Ray, with the creativity of the School. You will fall into the category of useful statues, but your inner ranges of perception will be local. I cannot understand how you manage to still hold out in the position of the man of the Path.

The man of the Path does not stand still, he constantly tries to follow the Hoopoe, even crawling when there are no other options.

Following the Hoopoe to Mount Kaph, to the bird Simurg, is perhaps the most important thing. But without performing the secret hermetic practices that Hermes Trismegistus spread throughout the entire Orion Ring, you will not be able to climb up to the Kingdom of Heaven.

Attar's poem 'Mantiq-al-Tayr' ('The Conference of the Birds') tells that the king of birds, Simurgh, who lives far away, beyond the seas and the mountains, in the centre of the world, drops one of his magnificent, magic feathers. And the birds, who are tired of worldly strife, decide to find not only the centre of the world and the feather, but also their king himself. They know that his palace is located on the distant Mount Kaph. At first, some birds show cowardice: the nightingale refers to its quivering love for the rose, the parrot to the beauty of his plumage, the partridge cannot part with its native hills, the heron - with warm swamps, and the owl - with dark ruins. But after all, they embark on a daring journey, overcoming the seven valleys and seas (seven passions). Many seekers of happiness desert, some perish. And only thirty birds descend on Mount Kaph. And when their vision opens, they suddenly realize that they themselves are - Simurg, each separately and all together. For God is within ourselves.

The bird Simurg is the Heavenly Father, to whom the essence of the disciple who has embarked on the Path aspires, so that one day the disciple will find divine Love in his heart.

'I am the Way, and the Truth, and the Life,' (John 14:6) said Jesus Christ. If you can follow Him, living according to His commandments, you will become a man of the Way. Sometimes you manage to walk a little along the Way - to climb the spiritual ladder. But this path runs in your special states, in special higher zones of your consciousness. It consists in opening the spiritual heart and experiencing the highest love for the Creator of the Universe and us, love for your neighbours, and for all living beings.

When you will embark on this Path and gain awareness of your higher Self, then your face will be transformed into a countenance and you will be able to lead others along the Path. A disciple who really embarked on the Path of salvation will never abandon it.

Only very courageous people can follow the path of Enlightenment, performing the practices of awakening every day. People who do not possess such courage can embark on this Path if they are under special protection of some higher power.

Above us there is a School Protectorate - a kind of shield, a spiritual veil. It is important for us to be practical and make a thoughtful use of it, as long as this veil is there.

Under its protection, it is much easier for us to perform the practices of awakening in order to once somehow come closer to the Creator of the Universe. The veil works even for those in the School who live and act mechanically.

Many people make heroic efforts to find the School, but often pass by the truth that lies nearby. This happens because they already have an incorrectly crystallized point of view on what the Path should be and how to follow it.

To embark on the Path of salvation, you need to work hard on yourself.

Chapter 6. The search for a spiritual Master. The task of the wandering of the Master and his disciples in the outside world. A new etheric initiation. The parable of the invisibly growing seed

The disciple-adamite felt that another mental wind was blowing in the space around him. The wind of alchemical ideas, which is more promising for his climbing than his entire previous life.

And although the search for the Master in the labyrinths of life is very difficult, they show the logic of a person who wants to embark on the Path.

If nowadays a person has a strong desire to find similar opportunities, he will be able to find them in our small company, which travels all the time. Our company thus paves the way for the future man of the Path. We know how to move both outwardly and inwardly and we are aware of its value, but we, in principle, are not dependent on this outward movement. Inward movement comes as the result of our efforts in performing the practices of awakening: these are progress in spiritual development and the growth of our essence.

But in the given situation we move outwardly too, and this is of great importance for the whole country, for the planet earth, for the solar system. Because we establish a connection between the area in which we are present, with the highest spiritual universal Schools, the influences of the highest humanity. Thanks to this, the junction of many civilizations and many era's, new mystical magnets come into being, which will help people to embark on the path of spiritual development and resist the world chaos and the influences of infernal schools.

Try to recall what kind of person you were before entering the School? You couldn't even tear yourself away from your home, from the horizontal life. It was like a heroic deed for you just to stay in Moscow for a few weeks, to meet my disciples and to partake in the teaching situations, so that they melt you a little and temper you existentially. Look how case-hardened and grown up on the level of being you are now, after only seven years! Through our influence, atmosphere, faith, passion, labour, selfless devotion, sacrifice, mission, a new etheric Initiation of the mysterious Ray, bringing a message from hitherto unknown higher worlds, is realized in the history of the Earth.

There have been engraved on the rocks in Vyborg the symbols of several universal spiritual Schools. Now they radiate emanations of the etheric initiation into this area. It is therefore important to follow the changes in the etheric atmosphere, for new kinds of School radiation, strive not to create holes in the School's alchemical cauldron, through which all subtle energy will flow away into the chaos of life, into entropy.

The holes are: your pride, sense of self-importance, self-pity, condemnation of others, self-justification and rejection of the Master's corrections. Having such holes, no disciple can develop spiritually in the School space.

We are an incarnated alchemical school, although not one of our fellow-men believes this, even think of this being possible. Perhaps this situation will remain unchanged until the end of our days. This should not disappoint us, we should not inflict ourselves upon disciples who will sooner or later fall away. Although, this does not mean refusing to work with any person who shows interest towards us.

You both, working along the second line, sow spiritual seeds in the souls of disciples, but you cannot know in advance whether they will bear fruit. It depends only on the efforts of the disciple himself whether he will acquire spiritual gold, that is his higher nature and whether he will find in his heart the love for the Creator of the Universe. We are obliged to help all those seeking spiritual freedom, but where exactly they will come in the afterlife, when their incarnation has reached the end, depends on them.

Chapter 7. Conscious suffering or how to deal with inner temperature

Frunze, Palace of Sports

Kasyan: 'I asked G why it was necessary to consciously endure the psychological pain of his admonitions, which constantly arises at the slightest of his comments, and to carry a heavy load of negatives of other students on our shoulders.

All this is necessary, replied G, to acquire the alchemical fusion in our team, and for this one must consciously endure everything. Why has it become much easier in our country than before? Because a continual fusion is going on.

Alchemical fusion is of great importance and for the sake of it we must endure mental pain and suffering. For this is the only way to change something in the world around us, also in Panicovsky and Gouri. No one besides us, would want to go for it.

Inner temperature is a very painful matter. Therefore, when it rises, the disciple forgets the doctrine, and there remains only inexplicable pain because of the seeming injustice or resentment. Raw spots of our soul and astral body generate a false interpretation of all the events that take place, both in the School and in everyday life.

The disciple must realize that it is not his physical body that is melted, but his soul, and therefore the attacks of pain are unusual, inexplicable and almost unbearable.

The soul of an ordinary person is not prepared to the perception of the higher worlds, it is uncompleted, not processed by fire, and therefore the School cares for the alchemical melting of the inner composition of the disciple. Therefore, pain is inevitable and must be endured consciously and deliberately. The main thing is not to let pain make you lose what little was left of your mind.

The disciple must deeply realize that when he wants to accuse the Master of injustice, it's a sign that the alchemical temperature has risen.

What can be done in regards to the increased temperature? Your best bet is to find a quiet place, and throw out all your claims on paper, and then burn it. Then the negative will be separated from you and you will observe at a distance how your immature holodains mumble all sorts of nonsense. And then, reconsider your discontent and go to church, and say prayers of forgiveness for the Master and fellow-disciples of the School. Then negative emotions and pain will abandon your soul.

Not to neglect alarm signs for the disciple must be when he feels his feeling of self-importance growing and he cannot restrain his pride from negative reactions to the admonitions of the Master or elder disciples. Those alarm signs mean that his bad karma has again substantially increased. And this means he must immediately go through the stage of purification over and over again, until the dregs in his soul subside, and his ego is back to its normal proportions, and humbly accepts the teaching situation.

The main task for a disciple under such circumstances is to transform all his negatives, remove them from the heart and get rid of the heaviness in the area of the belly, which presses on his neighbours and loads them with his heavy karma. Actually his task is to transform not only his own negatives, but also the negatives of his fellow-disciples and other neighbours and their karma and share with them the love of his heart. If he will not do this, then his malicious, cold subpersonalities and larvae will accumulate hatred, and will put a huge axe under his spiritual compass, which will quickly lead him away from the Path of the Enlightened Ones into horizontal life and then in chaos.'

Chapter 8. How to burn the infernal traits and cultivate noble ones. About initiatory literature. About the sensitivity of the heart. The subtle atmosphere in the School helps the disciples to grow

27th April 1987, Alma-Ata, hotel "Kazakhstan", room 1414

We need to be able to burn all the infernal traits of people's character, which in Christianity are called sins, that is pride, vanity, resentment, anger, condemnation. Because many people are doomed to possess infernal traits: when Lucifer fell, every man was saddled with a dark twin.
And our task is to cultivate the whole set of positive traits, such as faith, honour, love, mercy, compassion, humility, etc. and avoid falling into infernal pits and swamps.
Our next task is to be accepted in the universal spiritual Schools of light and to assert honour, steadfastness and will on the path of spiritual development. Honour means that if you made a promise to the Lord or to the Master that you will follow the Path of Enlightenment, then it will be a matter of honour for you to fulfil this promise, whatever it takes, overcoming all obstacles by your will and perseverance.

People in general believe that their passions and negatives are part of their character. In fact, the passions and the negatives are agents of the dark powers and dark powers act through them. Man forgot that he is a spark of the Absolute because his essence is asleep, and his false personality and uroboros rule in the inner kingdom. You on the contrary have precious knowledge about the structure of your soul, and about the constant struggle between good and evil inside man. By performing daily awakening practices, you are putting up resistance to your inner dragon, which is the personification of the infernal powers in man.

Climbing up along the Path of Enlightenment, you restore the lost connection with the Heavenly Father, so that later you can help the others to climb up.

In Bunin's novels you can find the whole range of positive as well as negative qualities of a person.
Similar inspiration was captured by two other Russians - Mikhail Chekhov and Konstantin Stanislavsky, and they were initiates. Nicolas Berdyaev was a knight and he was guarded by a high knightly circle. Mikhail Chekhov is one of the great initiates of the twentieth century, as well as Vladimir Shmakov. No one understood what these people introduced into the planetary culture. No one understood George Gurdjieff either. It is possible to understand the systems of Konstantin Stanislavsky, Mikhail Chekhov, George Gurdjieff only being in the alchemical School. Why did you manage to get to the bottom of this by yourself? Because you have grown spiritually enough to be able to see the School, and owing to the School, you see the depth of those teachings.

Nobody understands what Sufism is, even many Sufis do not understand it. Sufism can be understood only by an awakened heart, and not by reason or by a collection of certain codes, or by performing certain exercises. A disciple can grow when there is a fragile subtle being in him - his awakened essence. If this defenceless creature is not there or it is asleep, then the disciple cannot develop spiritually.
The heart should vibrate gently for everything, for all human manifestations.
The School creates a wonderful atmosphere for every student to grow. At first, your mediumship was dirty and nightmarish, unbearable for your neighbours... But you began to reconsider your 'horizontal' past, repent your sins and gradually it becomes still more pure. Undergoing of the Albedo stage helps to make the heart more sensitive

and perceive the energy of the higher worlds of our Heavenly Father.

Chapter 9. It is necessary to consider the influence of the external environment. On the importance of spiritual practices and stalking. Vertical creativity on the Ship of Fools

27th April 1987, Alma-Ata, the Palace of Sessions. Rehearsal

The cause of many troubles of the disciples is their inability to take into account the requirements of the external environment. They want just the opposite, that their environment would consider the disciples' opinion and position, and would approve their desire to follow the Path. But this is not real, because the disciples' are just a few, while the external environment consists of billions of people who live their shallow horizontal life and do not care a damn about the sense of self-importance of those disciples.

The biggest disciples' trouble is caused however by their inability to accept and to observe the admonitions and instructions of their Master, for his admonitions are always painful and are aimed at melting and strengthening the weak spots of the soul.

If a hostile external environment interferes with a disciple's spiritual practice, then it is necessary to improve his stalking. That is to consider the requirements of the environment and to improve his skills and tactics to such an extent so that his work on himself will not interfere with the environment. That is to work on himself in a discrete manner, not attracting the attention of the environment to his actions. The ability to consider the requirement of an external environment hostile to the Path of Enlightenment, means being able to exchange a normal, at least neutral feedback with it. The disciple needs also to improve his skill in establishing feedback with the Master and co-disciples of the School.

A person who enrolled in the School becomes a disciple only if he can humbly accept the admonitions of the Master, senior disciples and perform regularly the spiritual practices given to him for the sake of his development.

If a disciple forgets working on himself, then he quickly demagnetizes. Under the influence of horizontal chaos, its inner vector changes direction, the desire to restore connection with the Lord disappears, and his heart becomes filled with many conflicting, horizontal desires.

In order to hold out on the Path to the Kingdom of Heaven, the disciple needs to build a new character that allows him to continue work on himself under any given circumstances of life.

If the disciple will not abandon the Path, he will gradually open in his heart the highest love for the Heavenly Father and receive grace that will overshadow all earthly blessings.

The Master in the School specifies the framework, a kind of canon within which the disciple can create on his own. Vertical creativity should be canonical, without going beyond the framework of the School Ray. Creativity, which doesn't concern the tasks of the School, is not canonical and has nothing to do with the Ray. The disciple who wants to be engaged in canonical creativity must study the canon of the Ray for a long time, by undergoing various teaching situations. When a disciple's creativity goes beyond the School canon, the Master can make a correction in the disciple's behaviour.

Spiritual creativity is aimed at sharing with the world an impulse of light and purity.

However a disciple's reworking the practices of awakening in his own way is not creativity, but profanation and can be very harmful to the disciple's health or that of those who follow him. Practices of awakening were created by great teachers and tested by many generations of their disciples who, by diligently performing those practices, have achieved Enlightenment.

Chapter 10. How to come in contact with the collective soul of all Adamites? Who is Kulturträger? About the elevated essential relationships in the worlds of light

8th 1987, Almaty, Palace of Sessions, Arsenal's concert, 19:30

Today G raised an old topic of contact with Jus and Stirlitz, the two 'hares' with their own strange inner worlds. The Master once gave me the task to find my way into those worlds, and try to warm their sleeping essences with the warmth of my heart. I could not however fulfil this task, because in those times I was very stubborn, proud, selfish and wanted just the opposite, namely that they would find their ways into my inner world.

Master G sets before us the task of finding our ways into the inner worlds of all the members of the Adamic column and approaching the collective soul of all mankind, which is the Mother of God and Jesus Christ.

Christ is the new Adamic soul. This is the new leader, the new Adam Kadmon of the entire human column. We all must leave behind our old collective soul and join Christ. He is the One through Whom we can return to our Heavenly Father, for Christ, by His appearance on Earth, established a new Path of salvation for all mankind.

But man must make a choice by himself and by his own efforts join the new Adamic soul.

Hermes Trismegistus and Jesus Christ are our spiritual leaders, following in their footsteps, we can comprehend the essence of the Collective Soul.

Of course, it is very difficult for ordinary consciousness to assimilate the idea of compassion and the inevitability of learning the inner world of each person, each Adamite.

G says that each of us should become the spiritual leader of the underdeveloped blooming human souls. 'Imagine, you will be given a collective of people, or, for example, a country, and do whatever it takes to raise the spiritual and cultural level of its population. And you will be held accountable for those people before the higher spiritual authorities. If you are fine-tuned enough, then even being incarnated on Earth you can be in contact with various universal spiritual Schools.

To reach such a high level, you need to plead for the help of higher powers and perform the practices of awakening. You cannot accomplish this on your own. A close-knit team is required, a School that has a connection with the Heavenly Father, such a School can fulfil this task.'

Sometimes, I feel the touch of a subtle feminine being, which shows me what kind of elevated relationship exists between the human beings of a higher order. It is impossible to deceive anyone there, all our plans are in the aura and are easy to read. One person can place another one inside himself and experiences all his inner states.

Chapter 11. Architecture that balances heaven and earth. Freemasonry. How to become the one who follows the Path

29th 1987, Almaty, hotel "Kazakhstan"

A park, a manor is a balance between God, heaven, nature and man. The art of such a delicate ratio is conveyed in Japanese courts and in Russian estates.

Bazhenov, a great Russian architect, built magnificent palaces and parks, taking into account these relationships. Illuminated with spiritual knowledge, he used Masonic symbols in his works, reminding people of the Path of spiritual climbing. They can still be seen in the preserved buildings in Tsaritsyno. 'Radiant delta', an eye in a triangle is a symbol of the All-Seeing Eye of the Creator of the Universe; eight-pointed stars are a symbol of the eighth day of creation, which signifies the eternal life of the soul; double columns are a symbol of the passage to the higher worlds. Bazhenov was the member of a free-masonic lodge 'Latona' with N. Novikov as head of the lodge.

In the 18th century, Paris was the centre of culture and esotericism. All occult works were published in Paris, and Novikov published their translations in Russian six months later.

The French were caught up in the wave of passionarity, stirred up by Napoleon, who was Charlemagne in his previous incarnation. In the Middle Ages Charlemagne ruled almost all of Europe and therefore in his new incarnation he wanted to achieve the same. When Napoleon's army was defeated, some of the soldiers had to stay in Russia. They were panhandling on the streets of Moscow addressing passers-by: 'cher ami', which is translated from French as 'dear friend'. The Russians did not like them and called them by a bastardisation of this word which sounded as 'sharamyzhnik', which became thus a synonym for a pit tramp. In the same way a bastardisation of the word 'freemason' was made, that is 'farmazon' to designate a nihilist or a freethinker.

At the end of the eighteenth century, the French mystic Louis-Claude de Saint-Martin created a new mystical movement which got the name 'Martinism'. The main attention in this mystical tradition was given to meditation, immersion in heartfelt prayer, capable of establishing a connection with the Lord. De Saint Martin called this tradition "The Way of the Heart".

There is another spiritual tradition, close to Martinism, but older, Freemasonry. The name of it is derived from 'free mason'. The symbols of Freemasonry, which can be seen in many Catholic cathedrals, are the mason's tools: squares, trowel, compasses, plumb line and level, hammer and chisel, ruler and apron. These tools symbolize the spiritual building up of the human soul, which is in a destroyed state. A person who has fallen into the power of passions, sins, who has lost the 'vertical' guidelines leading to Enlightenment, is spiritually destroyed.

Since man inside himself, in his highest aspect, is the entire Universe, then the Universe is also in a destroyed state.

Why did the Freemasons call themselves 'free masons'? Being free means the right to choose. Now a person has a choice: he can fall into the pit of inferno or follow the Path of the Enlightened Ones and find divine Love in his heart.

The disciple builds a spiritual man out of himself. To do this, he undergoes various stages of alchemical transformation, including melting in retorts. Retorts are the School teaching situations. Each alchemical retort creates conditions to elaborate a certain noble quality, such as willpower and intent to achieve unity with the Lord.

In the nineteenth century all the Russian nobility were freemasons. The basic ideas of the freemasons are taken from the Gospel. Christ said: 'Destroy this temple, and in three days I will raise it up.' (John 2:19)

Nowadays, Masonry refers to various organizations that have little to do with the spiritual Path.

A person always has a choice: go upwards or downwards. Before the universal catastrophe, we could sail in the stellar worlds, and now we have to learn this anew. Now there is a School that teaches disciples to sail the sea of diversity of the Adamic Column, but if this is made known publicly, then the School will be immediately destroyed. Our main goal is to erect the temple of the divine human being from the destroyed state in which he is now.

All peoples have already lost their ancient ability of clairvoyance for the sake of creating their own self, individuality. This was a progressive step, before the coming of Christ. Christ brought the Good News that our self could return to God.

The atmosphere of the School Ray contains all the necessary elements for man's development; outside of this atmosphere it is very difficult to deeply immerse in oneself. When we arrive in a new city, we find always an atmosphere of chaos, stupidity, a break with the advanced ideas of higher humanity, which has moved into hyperphysical spheres. It is the atmosphere of the Ray that is the connection on the ideal plane of the given city with the advanced humanity of the extra-terrestrial civilizations. This connection is established through invisible atmospheric channels, through the plane of ideas, through the noosphere.

Adherents of the dark and grey currents, on the contrary, cut off all communication channels of humanity on Earth with advanced stellar civilizations, sentencing people to fall, to lag behind the new ideas, in other words, to lag behind the Spirit of our Time – the Archangel Michael.

Thus, our activity can be called a re-magnetizing of grey currents into currents of light, where human souls can develop themselves peacefully and naturally. It is possible to re-magnetize a person from one current to another in an alchemical, quick way, by bringing his soul in deep contact with one or all members of the School. But at the same time thus a collision of two opposite structures occurs and a strong internal friction arises, which is felt as a feeling of discomfort, apathy, chaos. Disciples must make a special super-effort to stop the erosion of their inner structure and restore it.

It can be seen from this that if a person has an incorrect inner crystallization, or if it has not yet been completed, then he will not be able to stay in the School for a long time due to the strong influence of negative centrifugal forces. These forces plunge a person into the chaos of the 'horizontal' world, with its many temptations and traps, lull the essence and pollute the soul. Therefore, it is so important for the disciple to get rid of attachment to passions, to reconsider his negative manifestations and false mind settings. This will allow him to humbly accept the Master's admonitions and endure the heightened psychological temperature during alchemical melting, without throwing it off in resentment, anger and self-justification.

Gradually, the soul will become case-hardened and acquire noble properties: love, mercy, compassion, and will also aspire to the Lord along the path of the enlightened ones. Then the disciple has a chance to enter the higher worlds at the front door.

Chapter 12. The era of rudeness and lack of culture. About the culture of everyday life

Beginning in 1917, an attempt was made to carry out the genocide of the entire Russian nation and to reduce the entire Russian culture to the norms of a banana republic. And the Russian nation has for its development its own language, its own religion. We are now witnessing the awakening of a giant from lethargy.

Having seized power, the lower castes rushed to implant their own culture, that is, the absence of it. Now we live in an era when no one knows what culture and nobility are. Rudeness and lack of culture are promoted and become the norm. This is a manifestation of the lower classes, which has swallowed everything. The period until 1917 is the top of culture to which the Slavs were brought. But then the boor and the commoner flooded our entire country with themselves, and only now we begin to wake up. What is shown in films about culture before 1917 is not culture, but a pitiful attempt by stablemen to play the role of a landlord. If you communicate with really cultured people, then you will always feel the difference.

A man of culture was e.g. Shulgin; Russians learned from him how to communicate properly with each other. There has never been such a lack of culture as now. People are doomed to disorder in everyday life. These uncultured traits crystallize in youth and it is difficult to fight them. The whole culture can degenerate due to rudeness which has become a norm in society. We must train ourselves to maintain order both inwardly and outwardly.

The question of everyday living conditions is a difficult question, when you focus on it, you immediately begin to remember yourself. Living conditions concerns the deepest part of you. It manifests itself at work, at home, it is inseparable from you. An atmosphere of harmony should always radiate around you. While your rooms in hotels always smell of dung, silage and stables.

The mystery of inner harmony is something which can be plumbed only gradually, you should meditate on this issue for a long time. But presently it is no longer possible to neglect your everyday life, which has crystallized into an infra-life. You both must focus on your living conditions, so that when entering your room, your guest could feel both outward cleanliness and an in-depth atmosphere in which he would wish to stay longer. This work is the basis of alchemy, to turn the lead of your chaos into at least the copper of order. Then the valuable and precious alchemical metals will emerge inside your soul too. Even if you are in the stable there will be still an elevated order present in your atmosphere. Now the School space for you both is your hotel rooms which you litter outrageously. And together we must maintain an atmospheric order at e.g. the railway station, concert halls, in the other picturesque places. We must learn to live as the upper class. Now we live in everyday life, like the pariahs, in the ultimate chaos. We must learn to be a man of labour, a man of trade, a man of the temple.

Chapter 13. Cultivation of subtle perception. Hermetic mind. The fusion of Hermetic and Christian currents. Creative experiment of the new chivalry

2^d May 1987, Moscow, Fairy's apartment

In order to come into the subtle worlds, the disciple must cultivate a vision of images. Various initiatory dreams come through images. The disciple might see in his meditations the flow of symbolic images. The section Pictura is a sub-section of the Ars section. Pictura is the cultivation of the perception of images, the ability to feel paintings. If the disciple has not cultivated the perception of images, he will be blind on the subtle plane. Each disciple has to develop an ear to hear, an eye to see and a heart to feel, so that he will not be deaf and blind on the subtle plane.
The disciple must be able to hear what ordinary people do not hear, discern various intonations of the Master, notice the subtle nuances of his facial expressions, certain gestures, be able to feel both the atmosphere of impending threat and of the Botticelli-spring. By understanding the sense of rhythm, the disciple gets past a complex system of the guardians of the threshold. Sound in the subtle worlds also plays an important role. When the disciple understands the system of imaginations, it means that he has deciphered the language of subtle entities.

There is a fallen mind and there is an enlightened metanoia. If we do not transform our fallen mind into an incorruptible reason, we will perish. The highest reason is given by Hermes in his teaching. We can comprehend hermetic ideas with our mind, clothe our mind with hermetic ideas. There is now an opportunity for us to undergo a hermetic metanoia, to clothe ourselves with mystical eidos. These are beings which spread ideas across all the sections and divisions of spiritual cosmic Schools.

If your little mind joins the circle of ideas of Hermes, it means that you are entering the ocean. Then you start collaborating with the stars.

Jesus Christ said: 'Do not think that I have come to loosen the law or the prophets. I have not come to loosen, but to fulfil.' (Matthew 5:17), and God gave the law through Hermes. This is already cosmic metanoia. All beings in the cosmos are included in the cosmic mind of Hermes, and your mind will become bright and life-giving. Hermes waited until his successor came in the twentieth century, and then Hermes left our Universe. Someone in the twentieth century took the place of Hermes in the Universe, and he must learn Hermes' laws plus apply his own creativity.

If you observe the laws established by Hermes, you can make your mind immortal by observing those laws. But our mind still consists of ideological corpses. In the Hermetic mind, on the contrary, all ideas are alive.

The person that has taken the place of Hermes is faced with the most difficult task of realizing the fusion of two different currents - the Hermetic and the Christian ones. The first current is of cosmic reason and law, universal justice, while the second one is the current of compassion and all-forgiveness. Prayer for the fallen creation, for anyone who is in a state of decline. This current in its full and most perfect form was given to the human column by the Lord Jesus Christ. The task of our School is to enter this current, to apply it skilfully in all life's circumstances, without abandoning it even for a single moment. If you are offended, and you immediately strike back a blow in your mind, then this is an action in the current of old Adam, that is 'an eye for an eye, a tooth for a tooth'. But if you do otherwise and do not strike back, then you will see how your old Adam is crucified on the cross when you try to act in the current of the New Testament. And if you have even partially embarked on this path, then this is what you have been seeking for ages, and this is the hope for you and your loved ones.

You can already combine your tiny achievements in this current with the results you have achieved already on the hermetic ladder of ascent. Your strength may not be enough to steadily climb the hermetic ladder of ascent, which was created for heroes, titans, martyrs. You might not be them, you may not pull on the Hermetic path of ascent. But if you are filled with the current of the New Testament then a miracle happens. You suddenly find the strength and ability to climb along the harsh path designed for heroes. You, being by nature an ordinary person, begin to join cosmic humanity, consciously or unconsciously. Hence it follows that the task of the spirit of our time consists in the harmonious synthesis of the Hermetic and Christian traditions, the synthesis of these two currents. The new chivalry sets up a creative experiment. But in order to harmoniously combine these currents, it is necessary to equally master both currents. Let your motto be the Gospel's words: 'The kingdom of heaven has endured violence, and the violent carry it away.' (Matt. 11:12). As long as you have enough strength, you must use all of it for inner growth in both currents. Because sometime in the future your power will be gone, do not think that you have a lot of time in stock, the deadlines are set for everyone.

Presently you can still study the hermetic impulse by filling your faded hearts with the eternal fire of the heart of Christ.

Chapter 14. About Fairy and G. White and Black Initiations. On the Hermetic Initiation. Hermetic knowledge is protected. How to avoid switching to the dark current

Moscow, KSB, 22:00, before departure

Fairy is like a liquid crystal: when the alchemical temperature inside her rises, she begins to boil, like sodium in water. Unable to stand in such an atmosphere for more than an hour, I run away. My mind loses its strength and all my spiritual magnets are demagnetized. G can come in such a state of boiling crystal during prolonged house arrest at Fairy's place.
G has at least three distinct inner states:
- incredible kindness and mercy of the right column: love for every person, all-forgiveness and all-understanding;
- the state of the left column: hermetic mercilessness in the sense of the law, when his words become heavy, like the hand of a knight;
- boiling lava of a raging volcano: if you get in the way of his flame, he will reduce you to ashes at once.

The initiation of light is based on love, understanding and striving of the monad towards the collective Adamic soul, towards the Adam of the New Testament, the Lord Jesus Christ.
The initiation of darkness is built on a complete denial of the principles of the light, on violence, on self-assertiveness and power.
In the Hermetic initiation, the most important thing is magical stabilization in the light current, and only then - the development of other facets of your soul. The motto of Hermetic Initiation is 'Sic semper': amongst all kinds of temptations of life never abandon your Path of Enlighten-

ment and the goal of your incarnation: reaching the Kingdom of Heaven.

Being magically stabilised means not expressing negative emotions towards others, not falling into horizontal traps, controlling your passions, not falling in love so madly as to forget about God and the spiritual Path. Remember under any circumstances that you are a spiritual being and your goals have nothing to do with the goals of the body. Perform practices of awakening regularly regardless of external circumstances and mood swings.

We need to find our successors, disciples and form our adepts for the further consolidation of the School on planet Earth. There is also the problem of preparing the inhabitants of the Earth for the perception of a new initiatory impulse.

When the Triangle has a feedback on the heart-soul level, then wherever it goes, the powers of the cosmic Ray follow it.

Unibrogalia is a magical hermetic manuscript. Why? Apparently because it provides a decoding of the hermetic knowledge of our Universe, such manuscripts are studied in secret sacred crypts.

Any secret knowledge is guarded by the guardians of the threshold, these are certain magical powers, both of the light and of the darkness, which watch over those who study this knowledge or just make brief acquaintance with it. And if such an interested person is not worthy of this knowledge, the guardian of the threshold removes him from the physical plane through a catastrophe, accident, or something else. Therefore, when approaching hermetic manuscripts, one must know what kind of danger lurks behind them. And everyone who thinks to touch this knowledge harmlessly will suffer a severe fiasco. This can result in death or switching into a dark current, which is just as disastrous for those who try to follow the path of light.

Switching to the dark current always happens imperceptibly. A person becomes confident in his righteousness, becomes harsh, uses psychological violence against others.

While in the current of light a person feels joy and love for people. He always takes into account the opinion of his neighbours, can follow changes in their mood, listens to their opinion, never walks over people, but shows them mercy and compassion. Therefore, one must remember how the dark current differs from the light one and be watchful of himself so as not to allow manifestations of the dark current through him.

The disciple can never correctly assess his condition on his own. He does not notice how intolerance to the opinions of others appears in him, irritation, hypertrophy of his feeling of righteousness, his vision of the situation, increased anger, rage.

In order not to become a victim of the dark current, the disciple must humbly accept the admonitions of the Master and senior disciples.

Chapter 15. About how to properly train the disciples of the Ship. About one's work on oneself

21st May 1987 Moscow, Palace of Culture of Car Factory

Kasyan-Morose: 'My initial idea of the School was wrong, now I have to re-evaluate the principles on which it was based. That was the most harsh criticism of the new disciples, on their rapid upbringing to my hand, that is to bring them to observe the School rules, which sat in my head like nails. Gouri-Bitumen and I thoroughly tracked down all their faux pas and criticized them till they would break, and the incorrigible ones we tried to drive out of the School. This was, as it became clear for us many years later, an erroneous behaviour on our part. We had to protect the new disciples from the hardships of life, sympathise with them, wipe their tears and their nose and pull out their splinters, even while they would creak, whine, hate, count their pennies, make claims, meow and make pitiful grimaces. Now I know very well that I ought to love, empathize, care and praise them beyond measure. Approach them cordially and reverently.

To begin with, the new disciples need to be motivated to perform the practices of awakening that will help them grow spiritually. A disciple needs to gain his own vertical experience, then he will conceive his own desire to follow the spiritual Path, and there will be no need to force him to climb along the Holy Mountain.

If the disciple however decides that the Path of Enlightenment is not for him, he must be left alone. Hermetic knowledge is given only to a select few, those spiritual seekers who yearn to find a connection with the Creator of the Universe. One's work on oneself is a long-term process that can last a lifetime.'

8th May 1987, Simferopol, Palace of Culture of Builders, concert

G: 'Sharing atmospherically the energy of the Ray with the disciples of our School and analysing their situations is possible only when they join our Triangle at their ease. Pulling someone in forcibly, imposing obligations of spiritual development on someone is not our method, it will get us nowhere. It is good if a disciple can leisurely have a cup of tea in the atmosphere of the Ray, play backgammon, chess, feeling natural and confident, and stay with us of his own free will. We must be able to arouse his interest in the Ray of the School, in the teaching situations, in our spiritual goals. To create such an atmosphere, a number of efforts must be made and the foremost is: to pay more attention to the disciple than to yourself. At first, learn to take care of him as of a child, and if he becomes confused or negative from the sudden increase of the alchemical temperature, help him by explaining why this is happening to him. It is necessary to explain to the disciple how to clear karma, because it will determine how comfortable he will feel in our atmosphere. And also to explain that the atmosphere of the Ray melts those weak and raw spots of the soul like pride, vanity, jealousy, a sense of self-importance and other passions.

With all this, one must take into account the density of the atmosphere of the Ray coming from the Triangle onto the disciple. Here you need to hit the bull's-eye: both overshoot and undershoot are not allowed.

Before giving the disciple any lesson, such as e.g. an analysis of a teaching situation in which he participated together with an analysis of his mistakes and faux pas, it is necessary to create for him an entrance in our triangular magisterium. This is an entrance in the alchemical cauldron, in which there is always a heightened alchemical temperature. For no one can fit into it by himself at the proper level. It is necessary to open the gate of the cauldron and politely let the disciple in there. Then, having battened down all the psychological hatches, gradually begin to analyse his mistakes and teach him lessons and the good news through the teaching situation. I convey about ninety percent of my instructions and knowledge through situational training, not through lecturing.

Beware that if you apply too high a temperature to an unprepared disciple, he might run away from the Slippery Deck due to his wounded pride. He will fancy that he had been bullied and insulted, and will fall into an overwhelming self-pity. Only a Master can melt disciples to the right measure.

It is only against the background of Panicovsky and other new disciples that I can continue sharing with you practical hermetic knowledge. For you are no longer able to perceive the teaching inside our Triangle. Panicovsky has a keen eye for the delicate openwork of relations between disciples, which you no longer notice let alone give any importance to it. His keen eye is very useful for you and Gouri-Bitumen. The disciple is best affected by the Triangle atmosphere when all the three corners of the Triangle are present. If you tell a disciple about his mistakes one by one, then he often turns a deaf ear, he does not believe you. But when the volumetric effect of the Triangle's atmosphere comes onto the disciple, this atmosphere changes him regardless of his mood.

A clear algorithm for interacting with disciples is outlined. A new disciple comes to the School, with a 'horizontal' attitude towards the Triangle. Therefore he perceives all manifestations of the Triangle from a worldly point of view. Nevertheless, we need to establish a friendly relationship with him, and then create a situation of collective discussion of all his mistakes. It is necessary to start with determining the wrong patterns of his behaviour and his false mind settings behind those patterns. Then discuss his emotional experiences, and only then move to his subconscious level, where every disciple is always wild and crazy. When he learns to control his crazy instincts, then he will be ripe for his independent Brownian movements across the field of life and will be able to embark on the Path of Enlightenment, in order to once find in his heart the love for the Almighty.'

Chapter 16. How to pass the test by the powers of chaos?

22^د May 1987, Minsk, Palace of Culture Car Factory, 17:00

Kasyan-Morose: 'Today G said that we do not have to go into the abyss of chaotic worlds in order to learn to master chaos. Here we have Gouri-Bituimen and Fairy - two representatives of chaos, and you just need to learn to work with them. Such a task is given to a disciple who is capable of forming a crystal of his working 'self' so that he can hold his ground, even if being sent into the thick of chaos. Chaos would demagnetize him, invading his soul, his heart, his thoughts, his essence, reducing everything to ashes, demagnetizing all his acquired positive skills and qualities. Chaos is chaos, and the disciple must undergo various degrees of impact by the powers of chaos and withstand this negative chaotic current. And this means that I must find strength to endure mental pain, and restrain my dislike of the hostile origin in other disciples. Every day I must endure the poison that is released from Gouri in tons and not succumb to the provocations of his dark twin.

But chaos also demagnetizes me through intimacy with a woman who doesn't belong to the School, with a woman of the lower class. My working 'self' suffers a major fiasco then. Arjuna's working group becomes completely demagnetized through my close association with worldly women. Having lost the substance of the meaning of life, I lose inspiration and interest in spiritual development. To get rid of the heavy horizontal energies that drag me into the mundane swamp, I need to return to the practices of the stage of purification again and again.

Chapter 17. The refined atmosphere of the alchemical Ray. What does 'communication on the energy of the belly' mean? How to develop subtle perception

G: 'The atmosphere of the cosmic Ray seeps into the space of the School only through the Master and those disciples who are cordially and mentally tuned in to his inner wave. The School has a lot of comfortable sides, various kinds of euphoria, mental, and other kinds of pleasures, as well as 'hard currency' when the meaning of life of the concerned is striving for Enlightenment. But it is very difficult in such a situation to form yourself spiritually against the background of complete chaos of your fellow-disciples, without hurting their pride. The main thing is to keep modest in the School and not dominate the situation and the subtle School atmosphere, staying at the level of the spiritual heart. But the more the soul is polluted, the more difficult it is to observe this condition.

The disciple who communicates rudely and throws off his heavy karma into the common ethereal atmosphere, destroys it. Therefore, everyone avoids communication with him.

The disciple who is able to focus his attention at the level of his heart, is felt by others as an easy and joyful person in communication. He does not suppress anyone with his will, but, on the contrary, can provide friendly support.

Kasyan: 'I need to learn how to analyse our Ship's situation from all the facets of my slack-baked perception. And also gradually develop more advanced organs of perception. For example, learn to see myself not as a point in the space of life, but as a continuous timeline.

G said to me: 'Gouri is your stumbling block, he is watching you. If you go too far, do something wrong, communicate with him incorrectly, then you lose all your energy. And if you start to scare him, disparage him, then you yourself fall to the level of the beast. Gouri is a representative of elemental powers, you need to know how to handle him, because we need him badly for our cause.

Gouri contains heavy alchemical elements: nickel, oil and such like. If we kick him away, then we will start to get into trouble, while we could bring him up as a good rogue, a kind of Bertuccio, the servant of Count Monte Christo.

You must put aside your extreme demand to him, to make him choose definitely whether he is with us or against us. We must learn to balance over the abyss.

We cannot live on the slippery deck of the Ship according to the Old Testament commandment: 'an eye for an eye, a tooth for a tooth' and respond to negative with negative. Otherwise, we will only augment evil in this world, and the subtle energy we've amassed with such great difficulty will go into entropy. You will have to go through the stage of soul cleansing anew and patch up the holes in your energy cocoon made by anger, irritation, and resentment.

We have another goal: to give people love and joy. Christ gave his disciples a new commandment: 'Love one another. Just as I have loved you, so also must you love one another.' (John 13: 34)

For this is the only way to allow everything that is inside us to flourish and balance. Every scallywag and freak outside is a mirror of what is inside you and inside every person. Learn to forgive and transform the negatives of others through reconsideration, prayer of forgiveness, and sincere repentance of sins.

At the School you need to be able to find a common language with all disciples, because each of them is a reflection of you. If you cannot establish friendly communication with someone, it means that you do not accept part of your own soul or deny some of your own manifestations. It is very interesting to observe which disciples you dislike the most and why. Try to make friends with them, having tracked down in yourself those qualities that you dislike in others.

Every disciple has a chance of spiritual growth, of achieving a contact with the Lord. But only if he himself wants it and takes the initiative on the spiritual Path, performing the practices of awakening and purifying the soul. Then one day the fire of love for the Creator of the Universe will burn in his heart.'

Kasyan: 'I shouldn't bare my soul neither to Panicovsky, nor to Gouri, nor to Shurio, nor to girls, nor to anyone. But without shutting off my heart from them, rather by hiding my knowledge. I must learn to converse on any common topic, to understand what they need, to play any role that is acceptable for them, but not to give my soul to anyone.

I must be able to deftly disguise the process of my learning the spiritual knowledge. In our business, the main thing is to be modest and not to show off with knowledge or virtues.

In terms of Castaneda, I need to develop stalking that is to play various roles, but at the same time not to forget to follow the Path of Enlightenment.'

Chapter 18. Adultery is a crime. How to curb your instincts? Working with the ladies on the Argonauts' Ship

27th May 1987, Minsk, Palace of Culture of Car Factory
Kasyan: 'According to the laws of the Universe, entering into an intimate relationship with various women is a crime that is equivalent to theft or murder. It's just that now the morals of society have fallen so low that fornication is not considered to be a crime. But for those who embark on the Path of Enlightenment, it is imperative to know that in the Universe fornication is considered to be a crime of the same gravity as theft and murder. It is allowed to choose one woman, a wife, to be married to her and have an intimate relationship.

If you enter into an intimate relationship with a woman, then you take upon yourself her karma and the karma of all her lovers. Suddenly it becomes much easier for them to live, they become fortunate in life, and for you it is the contrary: life becomes harder and with less luck.

You can kiss, hug women, communicate with them on an astral level, but as soon as you have physical sex with them, that's it, you have committed a crime. This fact must be chiselled in my mind.

Intimate relationships strongly pollute a disciple's soul, as they link him to the lower astral. All his subtle energy that he has amassed and needs badly for performing the awakening practices, goes there. In addition, a multiple interweaving of his etheric fibres with those of the loved one follows, which leads to quarrels, scandals, mutual discontent and claims. Negative manifestations consume a lot of energy and lead a disciple astray. To regain inspiration, he needs to undergo the Albedo stage again.

The disciple can climb the Holy Mountain only by curbing his animal nature every time it stirs up, and he must make every required effort to become a spiritual knight.

The instinctive-motoric centre of man seeks to obtain bodily pleasures and does not think about Enlightenment at all, moreover, it acts much faster than other centres. Therefore a disciple needs to perform Taoist practices and energy locks (bandhas) 1-3 times a day in order to sublimate sexual energy. This will raise the energy to the upper centres, and store it into a special energy cauldron inside the body.

Gradually, all centres: intellectual, emotional and instinctive-motoric begin to act in concert and strive towards the highest goal, unity with the Lord. This means that the disciple is in control of his dark twin and can keep his mind, body and soul pure.

Chastity elevates the soul, directing all the thoughts and desires of the disciple towards the Heavenly Father, for the main goal on the Path is to achieve heartfelt contact with the Lord.'

A disciple may help the spiritual growth of one or another talented woman without having an intimate relationship with her. If he however, succumbs to the temptation which is always there, then he burdens himself and the School with her karma and the karma of her lovers. From this, the School gives a strong lurch from the spheres of the spirit to the earthly spheres, an extra ballast appears that hinders the development of other disciples too.

Working with a woman should be smooth and easy: first, the disciple needs to gradually remove the veil of earthly problems from her. However, the disciple alone, by his own strength only, is not able to cope with this veil: it will certainly crush and ground him, lead him away to the world of pleasure. Zabolotsky wrote a short poem on this subject, entitled 'The Death of a Hero', 'Strawberry rustles around the dead beetle, his tarsus's are spread in the grass, he used to have thoughts about this and that, But now they've been pulled out from him...' Admiral elaborated on this matter more than once in his ballads.

You will be forced to work.
In a hole as deep as the night.
You will tickle corpses
and the corpses will laugh,
always, for all ages, for all years!'

The disciple can free a woman from the veil of earthly problems by warming her essence, as well as by inspiring her to perform practices of purification and awakening. Then she will be able to embark on the spiritual Path, and, supported by advice and heartfelt warmth, strive for the Lord.

Chapter 19. About deep work on oneself and the benefits of physical labour. On the importance of mastering various professions

Panicovsky and other disciples get very annoyed when Master G says that someone who hasn't been carrying the heavy cases of Arsenal's sound equipment during at least several years will never understand the School. Only after this long-lasting, heavy labour the disciple can become a human being. Why? Because carrying heavy cases for a long period of time makes all the entities lurking in a disciple's lower chakras as well as in his will and emotional centres rise to the surface of his daily consciousness. Then the School works at identifying those entities and cleaning his Augean stables, bringing him another step closer to the status of man.

In the first year of carrying the cases, a disciple just vomits curses. In the second year, his gut grows hard, like that of a hungry wolf, in the third year he understands that the cases must be carried with a smile in his heart, and only in the fourth year his body becomes strong, and his psyche, hardened by carrying the cases, becomes more refined and rich, it is a kind of Spartan-like education of body and spirit. We got accustomed to each other and taught the creatures living in our instinctive centres to negotiate with each other. Gradually positive emotions appeared during our physical and mental labour, that meant harmonious work of the three centres simultaneously. The knowledge and fiery admonitions that we received from the Master was stored due to this hard work in the memory of our muscles and bones and therefore became not easy to forget, contrary to the knowledge in the head. However carrying the cases brings about positive changes only under the supervision of the Master.

It takes courage and patience to follow the Path of salvation, not everyone will take up the fight against his dark twin.
Many are looking for easy ways to achieve Enlightenment, but there are no such. The Path of the heart, the Path of Love, which the Ship of Fools, the School follows, is harmonious and effective for achieving the highest goal, the divine Love of the Creator of the Universe. But it requires daily effort on the part of the disciple.
Each profession hones only one facet of the rough stone of our being. Therefore, a disciple should change the field of his activity from time to time, to master a lot of different professions. To master, at least at an amateurish level, painting, acting, directing of the situations, house painting, skills of a set dresser, to try himself in various spheres of human activity. The disciple should hunt every day for the manifestation of the new subtle sprouts of new qualities in his soul and water the old ones with his attention. And also try to use prose, poetry, painting in order to share his experience of the etheric initiation, to master the theory and practice of Alchemy, that is the art of obtaining the spiritual gold. As Admiral wrote in his ballad 'Learn to swim':

Learn to swim, learn to jump
On the mother of pearl of flying fish
And the rotten mushroom of knowledge
will explode right in front of you, like an evil whim...

We need to seriously learn to swim in various mental waters, and also find a modern, successful form of transmission of the teachings.

The jazz bands are ringing, buzzing,
And the angry monkeys
Showing their mutilated mouths.
While I, a crooked and drunken one,
Call them to the oceans

And rain the flowers into their champagne...

Such is the fate of the Teacher-Herald of the etheric initiation on the planet Earth.

Chapter 20. About conflicts and points of tension. About passionarity and overcoming obstacles on the Path of salvation

Continuation of the lecture on 27th May 1987

G: 'Conflicts in the School are simply necessary, as without conflicts there will be no real growth of disciples. There are inner and outer conflicts. Disciples usually cannot resolve their inner conflicts and 'nurture' them for years, so that they grow to gigantic proportions. Inner conflicts often become transformed into outward ones.

But the fact is that the growth of disciples takes place at the moment of overcoming the conflict. The conflict creates friction, which is fire, and as consequence an increased temperature in the School. The School is in fact an alchemical furnace, Athanor, where the disciples are re-melted. Conflicts can be overcome only when the disciple undergoes alchemical purification. Otherwise, the conflict sinks into the subconscious and at some point the disciple will explode like a bomb, for no apparent reason.

Conflicts are inherent to the spiritual growth: when a disciple tries to climb the ladder to heaven one step higher, then immediately friction arises between him and his environment. At the same time an inner conflict rises in the disciple, that is between his inclination to seek comfort and his passionary striving to work on his spiritual growth. Anyway if there are no conflicts and their resolving, then there is no life, no running water, stagnation sets in in the disciple's soul.

Seeking a quiet life is actually sinking into the realms of hell, stupidity, dullness, idiocy, rejecting studying in the School. Striving for God is the spearhead of the spirit that strives to ascend to the spiritual worlds, while becoming heated to glowing from inner and outer frictions against obstacles that arise on the Path of Enlightenment. And until the soul is burnt out in this struggle, the spirit will not be able to dwell freely without being subjected to the earthly attraction. That what makes us experience earthly joys will burn up, and then love for the Creator of the Universe can arise in our heart.

Inner conflicts arise in us due to the collision of interests of our different 'selves' and the uncoordinated activity of our different centres.

For example, our emotional and intellectual centres are consumed with desire to find the love of the Lord, while our instinctive-motoric centre wants to enjoy bodily pleasures. In this case, in the morning the disciple eagerly performs spiritual practices, but in the evening he longs to fall into the arms of a foxy girl. If he cannot curb his instincts, he will lose a great deal of his subtle energy that he accumulated through the practices. In order to successfully advance along the Path of Enlightenment, a disciple must constantly cleanse his soul, as well as sacrifice his attachment to the passion of lust.

Another inner conflict arises when a disciple's false personality prompts him to strive for horizontal happiness, career, various cultural and bodily pleasures, while his essence strives to find the love of the Creator of the Universe. In order to prioritize correctly, the disciple must be honest with himself that is to see clearly what's going on inside him. If there is a negative reaction to correctional comment of the Master, then there is a wrong mind setting or behaviour pattern that provokes an inner or outer conflict. The disciple can discover and eliminate the 'root' of his negative reaction using the exercise of reconsideration.

When a disciple overcomes obstacles arising on the Path, his soul matures, and his being grows both horizontally and vertically. He should not be afraid of problems and difficulties, run away from them into horizontal comfort that ruins the soul. All difficulties are a gift of the Lord, they are given according to the disciple's strength.

Chapter 21. About the struggle between the higher and lower vehicles of human monad. About the inner battle

Continuation of the lecture on 27th May 1987

There is an eternal mortal struggle between the various vehicles of the human monad: between the physical and the astral ones; astral and causal ones; causal one and the Higher Self.

A disciple, having embarked on the path of ascent, becomes the arena of the struggle for survival between his vehicles. The fact is that coarse vehicles live off the energy of subtle vehicles.

The human monad, descending into the depths of Malkuth from the spheres of Ain-Sof, that is from the spheres of the Heavenly Father, is sequentially clothed in eight vehicles, which are its mode of existence in the different spheres of existence. And so, climbing from the spheres of Malkuth to the spheres of Keter, man is confronted with a sharp battle between each lower and higher vehicle. In this battle, the higher vehicles try to subdue the lower ones, and the lower ones try to subdue the higher ones. The severity of the situation lies in the fact that the human monad is always clothed in several vehicles - shells, and in order to successfully advance along the Path to Climb, it will have to master all shells at the same time, seizing leadership over them. And then subject them to service for God and co-creation with Him. The monad must feel its closeness to God at all levels of divine creation, divine worlds, in all its shells.

A disciple who has embarked on the Path of Enlightenment wages daily inner warfare. For the spiritual growth of his essence is hindered by the dark structures of the soul. It is important to remember that man cannot climb to the Kingdom of Heaven on his own, without God's help.

Chapter 22. About the alchemical crucible of the soul and about alchemical melting. On the work of the Ship of the Argonauts in the sephira Malkuth

In order to master his vehicles, the disciple must create in himself an alchemical, tightly sealed crucible and let the 'raw', 'ore spots' become smelted by the secret, heavenly fire and transformed into the semi-precious and precious metals, insoluble in cosmic chaos, indestructible by dark forces, that is acquire stable positive qualities.

This work of the disciple must take place in the School atmosphere, under the supervision of the Master.

When climbing the Holy Mountain, the disciple is alternately exposed to the influence of the 'dead' and the 'living' water, to the influence of dark powers and to the influence of the philosopher's stone of Master G. The disciple perceives those influences indirectly, as his outer and inner conflicts, as his mental breakdowns, hysteria, volcanic-like emotional eruptions and such.

Subtle energy of the alchemical Ray from the higher worlds fills and revives the essence of the disciple. In order to transform the disciple's will centre and the instinctive-motoric centre, the Master acts as a severe benefactor, while working on a disciple's emotional and intellectual centres as the loving teacher. The Master raises without hesitation his spear over the disciple's dark twin, dealing from time to time a merciless blow to the seven-headed dragon, helping the disciple to overcome the dark part of his soul. At the same time, he lovingly supports the disciple's 'working group of Arjuna' and the essence of the disciple, instructing them how to follow the Path of Enlightenment.

In the hermetic cauldron of School teaching situations, the disciple's soul is gradually melted. As a result of alchemical transformation, he begins to understand how to separate the coarse from the subtle inside him. A hermetic crucible means that there are no holes in his soul through which subtle energy would flow away. Holes appear through pride, self-pity, resentment, condemnation, and other negative emotions. With other words these are the weak points of the disciple, which slow down the process of smelting of the precious alchemical metals, that is positive qualities. In order to mend the holes in his soul, the disciple needs to go through the purification stage.

The ability to manoeuvre in the alchemical sea comes with the years spent sailing on the Ship of Fools. Our triangular Magisterium sails in the alchemical waters of Malkuth, that is the manifested world. Its path is mysterious and unknown, dangerous, full of exciting adventures and quests. The task of the triangular Magisterium is to trigger off, through its homeopathic influence, an alchemical reaction in the Malkuth, in order to involve Malkuth in the stellar spiral of spiritual evolution.

Our School is backed by the mighty powers of the Ray H, the spearhead of the advanced Adamites of our Universe.'

Chapter 23. On the problems of magnetization and demagnetization. About conscious work on yourself. On the highest Sephirah of the Tree of Sephirot

1988, Simferopol, Hotel 'Moscow'

All disciples of the School have to cope with the same crucial issue: how to become magnetized by the ideas of the School? How to preserve and to grow the small sprouts of new ideas and designs in their soul, so that they become stronger and become eventually their new qualities. How to preserve the impulse of the School in their soul, how not to lose it being flooded by the chaos of life?

Soon after the disciple is left on his own, he becomes demagnetized and loses the momentum of the School, turning into a common person similar to people in his environment.

To prevent this, he needs a link to the School and performing spiritual practices on a daily basis. If however the link is weak, passive, then the disciple can lose the momentum while even being in the School. In order to preserve it he must be active along the three lines of School work.

As soon as the disciple is inactive, he immediately begins to demagnetize. He is always in danger of becoming a statue, a graveyard of ideas. Passive stay of the disciple's body in the School does not bear fruit: specific activities within the School are required.

Conscious work in the School, on a given topic, is called magnetization by School ideas, School work. For the completeness of schooling, the disciple must work along the three lines:

- work along the first line, that is the disciple's work on his spiritual growth: performing the practices of awakening and cultivating Christian virtues;

- work along the second line, that is work with fellow-disciples, helping them on the Path of Enlightenment;
- work on the third line, that is under immediate guidance of the Master along a strategic direction.

Working along the first line cleanses the soul, rids it of chaos and heavy karma and nourishes the essence with spiritual oxygen. It spreads so to say the sails of the soul to catch the spiritual wind. The School Ray gives inspiration, turns life into a fairy tale, a mystery that is inaccessible to a horizontal person. The Ray enables the disciple's essence to make a significant leap in spiritual evolution. Therefore, it is so important to appreciate the possibility of being on the deck of the Ship of Fools, the support of the Master and the subtle energy of the mysterious Ray.

The Master of the School maintains contact with the advanced part of the Adamic column, with the cosmic humanity which lives in the hyperphysical world. On the physical level of being the School is located in the sephirah Malkuth, at the very bottom of the universe. Advanced cosmic humanity lives in the upper sephirot. The ten worlds of the Sephiroth Tree represent ten hyperspheres of the habitation of living beings. Man can dwell in his astral body in one of these worlds, depending on the degree of his spiritual development: the higher the spiritual development of a person, the higher sephirah he can dwell in. The more polluted the karma of a person, the lower worlds he lives in and the stronger is his bondage there, the further away he is from God. The worlds of Malkuth are our manifested Universe, and the physical body is the most coarse vehicle of our monad.

A disciple needs a long period of study at the School until he can climb along the Sephirot tree to the level of Keter, to the level of the Messiahs of the entire Universe, of all the worlds of the Sephirot tree. Then, in the worlds of Keter, the adept becomes a conscious co-creator with the Lord and dwells in grace-filled joy, realizing that the Lord fills the entire Creation with Himself and at the same time He dwells in the heart of the adept.

This kabbalistic theory is not understandable to all inhabitants of the worlds of Malkuth. This riddle cannot be comprehended by an ordinary mind, it is understandable only to a pure heart and an enlightened mind.

Chapter 24. About subtlety and coarseness of the soul. About the styles of behaviour

1988, Simferopol, Hotel 'Moscow'

Rudeness, vulgarity and boorishness are manifested in a person due to the lack of aesthetic education, understanding of beauty in clothes, words, behaviour, art of painting, actions, deeds. Man must acquire a taste for beauty and harmony in everything. The gesture, the gaze, the intonation, the atmosphere of the person are important. To achieve all this, painstaking work is necessary in all spheres of life:
1. In painting, you need to learn at least schematically to draw in several styles: Chinese, European Gothic, especially Flemish, Byzantine.
2. You need to master the art of the spoken word, feel the structure of its sound, to have a well-trained voice, clearly express your thoughts. Learn to write poetry and prose that awakens the interest of the reader. Also learn to write in various alphabets - Latin, Greek, Chaldean, Tibetan. These, at first glance, simple things change very much, align the power lines of our being.
3. Next, you need to master the following styles of behaviour:
- the style of a London dandy: an aristocrat with sophisticated manners and refined language, elegantly dressed with a flamboyant style;
- the style of a Parisian beau: fashionably dressed gentleman, courteous, connoisseur of good manners and etiquette;
- the style of an adventurer: alert, not attached to comfort, not staying long in one place, able to adapt to any conditions, able to find a way out of any situation;
- the style of a Russian nobleman: honour, valour, patriotism, dignity, loyalty, education;

- the style of a knight: capable of waging daily inner warfare against his passions, not indulging in self-pity, cultivating the noble qualities of the soul, and also helping fellow-knights on the Path of Enlightenment;
- the style of a monk: striving to keep the heart and soul pure, to live according to the commandments of the Lord Jesus Christ, to be humble, to cultivate mercy and compassion in the heart, to love the Lord and to strengthen faith in Him;
- the style of Don Juan: to master the art of flirting with ladies, please them, pay attention, make compliments.

Style can only be developed on the basis of a subtle taste.
Rudeness, boorishness, arrogance - this is not a style, but manifestations of the animal level. It is necessary, on the contrary, to develop in oneself a Christian trait, meekness. In any tensed situation, do not curse anyone, restrain your anger and do not shout. This will be true work on the style of behaviour. Let the whole world curse me, but I should not sink to the bestial level of those cursing. Jesus said: 'Follow me, and allow the dead to bury their dead. (Matthew 8:22)

Chapter 25. About the alchemical songs of Admiral. About the fallacious philosophy of Panicovsky

Kasyan: 'Quite recently, in the Crimea, I began to feel the alchemical atmosphere of Admiral's songs, their otherworldly depth. The one who possesses the alchemical keys to his songs, can find a deep mystical meaning in each line of them.

Admiral, quite consciously, artistically and romantically, set out in his ballads a compendium of metaphysical doctrines in order to make them available to his followers. In his ballads, the bottomless depth of the white goddesses and hermetic knowledge can be found. Plunging into the atmosphere of his esoteric underground, you gradually find yourself in the magical world of the Holy Mount Kaph and, enjoying the reflections of the plumage of the king of birds Simurg and brilliance of the crystal castles of transcendental heights. G said that Admiral learned to split the meaning of words into atoms. But a coarse soul will not feel anything in his sparkling ballads. Admiral is the alchemical genius of the twentieth century. The etheric initiation that he received from G can be felt only by the refined soul and fiery heart, it cannot be grasped with the mind or touched with the hands.

Panicovsky, aka Rikki-Tikki-Tavi, is G's former disciple in his incarnation in India. He received this nickname for his speed of orientation and building useful contacts among the artists and the administration of the jazz ensemble 'Arsenal'. G demanded from Gouri and me that we would learn from Panicovsky his psychological techniques for quickly getting in touch with any person useful for the School. But it turned out to be above our strength because we got stuck in a reciprocal hostility, quarrelling who of the two of us is G's best disciple. We forgot that G needed a close-knit mystical team, not a scattered bunch of feuding would-be disciples. It was unthinkable for us to be friends with such a two-faced person as Panicovsky, who could always get us in the wrong in G's eyes, and have a free ride at our expense. Being wiry and hardy, Panicovsky, nevertheless, left the loading and unloading of the heaviest cases with apparatus to me and Gouri-Bitumen. He joined in companions to G, whom Gouri and I allocated the lightest boxes, because of his age and health problems. Travelling on the Ship of the Argonauts, disguised as 'Arsenal' technical crew, through the expanses of the Soviet Union, Panicovsky, returning to Moscow after the tour, each time would say: 'The city A has given me a present, and the city B too, but the city C did not understand me and has not given me a present, that is a night of love with a beautiful lady.' This fallacious philosophy swept him off his feet all the time. Being adhered to it, Panicovsky has loaded himself with horizontal karma over his head. And instead of flying on the energy of the Ray to heaven, he sank more and more into the swamp, taking upon himself the karma of his beautiful ladies, their lovers, and the karma of the lower astral layers of the cities. After that, he would fall into chaos and dullness of perception for a long time, not noticing the fantastic patterns of the School's life. Having lost, along with the substance of the sense of life, all his subtlety and charm, he was following us in the rear through the cities with a chilled heart and a stone-like face, muttering to himself: "Why does no one respects me, not love me and not pay attention to me?' He seemed to himself being still alive, but to us - already dead.

Panicovsky still felt like a Komsomol leader, which he was in the past, and believed more in horizontal life than in God, so he did not even think to limit his sexual appetite and to pray for the forgiveness of his sins instead. Although, he could have regained freshness of perception, joy in his heart and lightness in his soul, if he had not worshiped life, considering it a 'great teacher'. G was only a small part of his interests. Whereas for Gouri and me, G was the Master who led us to Enlightenment.

Why do we, disciples, not listen attentively to the sounding of the Ray in our inner and in the atmosphere around us every day? We put this off until tomorrow, which almost never comes, making efforts in self-transformation and the passage of the Albedo stage. And every day we solve a multidimensional koan: what it means to be 'alive' and what it means to be 'dead' for the School. 'Separate the subtle from the coarse in yourself, daily doing hermetic work,' - taught Hermes Trismegistus. And we hear his words and do nothing. Where can we find the willpower to perform the practices of awakening? Saint Seraphim of Sarov used to instruct his followers: 'If you do not want to do evil, then fear God and restrain yourself from doing evil; and if you want to do good, then fear God and do good.'

Chapter 26. How to get rid of loutish behaviour and reach the essential level of communication? How to cultivate courage

Kasyan-Morose: 'G decided to deepen our concept of loutish behaviour. He said that loutish behaviour is, next to plain rudeness, an indifferent, heartless, mechanical attitude towards a person too. Hypocrisy and pharisaism are also elements of loutish behaviour.

Courage is the ability to adhere inwardly to the ideal of a noble person and to be able not to fly off at a tangent into hypocrisy or loutish behaviour during the day.

A disciple, who follows the path of enlightenment is a warrior, a knight. Courage can emerge only when there is an inner heightened alchemical temperature, and the disciple withstands it. If there is no inner heightened temperature, then there is no reason for courage to be manifested.

All the criticism that you receive is an excellent means for your upbringing. Due to the sharp criticism of Panicovsky, you can work on cleansing and transformation of your filthy gut.

Loutish behaviour is a triumph of natural instincts. Our soul carries within itself both Hell and Paradise. If a disciple allows meanness to come into his soul, it kills his intuition, destroys his essence, pollutes him with bad karma, feeds his dark twin, uroboros and false personality. And to become cold in thoughts and evil at heart is already a fall.

If you both want to become transformed, then you need to find by feeling a certain centre of rudeness and loutish behaviour inside you and start working on it. Then gradually your simple faces might turn into countenances.

Sincerity is courage. Feedback between disciples in the School is also courage.

Quite often it happens that the centre of rudeness and loutish behaviour in a disciple remains unaffected by his work on himself even until his declining years...

If a person seeks to find contact with the Lord, he will have to take the path of enlightenment, and in order not to wander from the track, he needs to have enough courage. That is, to reach the essential level of communication, to take care of his fellow-disciples, to maintain the team spirit, to get rid of a sense of self-importance, to show others mercy and compassion. As long as the disciple is selfish and does not care for others, there will be no genuine joy in his life.'

Chapter 27. About Master G. When the Soul is Shrouded in Darkness. Do not Postpone the Performing of Spiritual Practices until Tomorrow. How to Cultivate Willpower

11th June 1987, Kiev, Palace of Culture of Korolev, 19:30, concert

Kasyan: 'We have been waiting for him for a long time. The old manuscripts told about him, and now, Master G has incarnated again, he is with us, he is among us. But, until now, he is not understood, alone, as if no one needs him. Now it is clear that he came from the higher worlds, while we have been incarnating all this time just here, on Earth. Follow him, accept his teachings, understand the good news that he brought. Will there be brave men among us? It is inspiring to read about the heroes of the spirit, sitting in comfort with your beloved. But who is ready to follow the Master in all verity: into the unknown, into conscious suffering, to follow his teaching goes against everything that we have heard before.

We wanted to ascend to the higher worlds as we were, rough and uncouth. For his care we paid him back with distrust, for the hope he gave with disappointment. From his admonitions we fell into self-pity and resentment. G used to say that he leads us towards the light and that only heroes can easily follow this path. And often I had nothing to say in return, because I indeed ranked below the level of hero. Learning from the Master was very difficult for us and sometimes we wanted to return into the world for a short respite.

Almost all my life I was looking for someone who would show me the way to the Holy Mountain. I found the Master in my thirties, it was G and I began to follow him. Later I followed him as a father, out of a desire to help him in his incredibly difficult mission, later on as a comrade in arms;

sometimes out of self-pity, sometimes out of compassion for him. He is the one who conveys the rays of the Divine sun, in whose company one always feels good and at the same time it is infinitely difficult. He embraces everything with his spirit, although he is poor and sometimes has nothing to eat. Sometimes, he is merciless and harsh towards his disciples, like Genghis Khan, at other times he is merciful, like the God of love and compassion.

For a long time the spirit of freedom has not awakened in me; for a long time the strings of my heart, which longs to find inside it the spiritual sun, filled with Love, have not sounded.

For a long time, dark thoughts sowed darkness in my heart, and my soul cried and pleaded God for enlightenment, but the heavens remained silent, and dark thoughts still swirled like clouds, hiding the sun in my soul. Darkness enveloped the soul and an empty nothingness came. The people around were sceptical about the good news, but it's as if have been weeping stones when the Master's heart would open for a while, and shared heavenly inspirations with us. But when he would fall silent, my heart shut off again, and the birds no longer sang in the serene sky, but only the black crows croaked on the wet branches. I wanted to breathe in the life-giving spiritual oxygen of the higher worlds of light again, instead of the cyanide vapours of Lucifer. But my heart kept silent, having become covered with mould. The time of spiritual joy ended, and the time of demonic sorrow had come. G looked into my sad eyes and said that I must direct my gaze upwards and began to perform the practices of awakening, combining them with ardent prayer to the Lord. And having cleansed my heart, I threw off the burden that caused passive resistance to alchemical transformation, and ascended to my spirit, which shines eternally in the heavenly heights.

It is necessary to take a step forward towards the top of the Holy Mountain every day, overcoming spiritual inertia with the help of hermetic practices and stalking.

But often my conscience sleeps soundly, because I am too lazy to transform myself, to make efforts and super-efforts in working on myself. I often forget that I am in the company of a mysterious Master who radiates spiritual light.'

Chapter 28. About the mission of the Lord Jesus Christ. About the Universal proclamation brought by G

12th June 1987 Kiev, Palace of Culture Koroleva, 16:00, rehearsal

Kasyan: 'In the morning we watched a six-hour film about the life of the Lord Jesus Christ at the Kiev 'hares' nicknamed Cacti. While watching the film Master G was at the same time recalling his then incarnation: he knew the great Messiah personally and saw Him dying on the cross. When he watched the scene of the crucifixion, tears appeared in his eyes. 'At those times,' he remarked, 'many adepts of Unibrogalia incarnated on Earth in order to receive the Divine message from the higher worlds.'

After the film, I deeply realized that Christ is God Who contains the whole Universe in Him. He took upon Himself the burden of the sins of the Earth and dispelled them with His sacrificial love. He embraced with His fiery heart all of humanity inhabiting the eighty-eight star systems of the Ring of Orion.

Two thousand years ago, the Son of God was born on Earth, and there were no royal receptions for Him, but only a group of disciples and believers in Him and the laity supporting Him, and Jewish priests who envied Him and tried in every way to denigrate Him. Life around was the same as now. The demon-possessed Israelite high priests recognized Him as a dangerous rival to their power and, therefore, by intrigue forced Pilate to crucify Him.

Now the School, linked to the Universal initiation, has incarnated on Earth, but people around look down on it, they only care about their own life.

The film well shows how unobtrusively, without solemn rituals, Jesus chose His apostles, we must understand and accept this: the apostles simply heard the call of His mouth and heart and showed their will and followed Him. Nowadays, those who have met the School can feel with the pure heart the message from the highest spiritual heights and follow it. But few people follow, for the heart does not feel the call of heaven, and the ears do not hear the spiritual message.

G, our Master, brings the cosmic proclamation to all corners of Russia, but these are mostly stones and spirits that listen to him. Why is man so abnormal, deaf to any word coming from God, and so sensitive to the desires of the body? G is the successor of Hermes in the Ring of Orion, his task is to unite two impulses and initiations, those of Jesus Christ and Hermes Trismegistus. G combines in himself the two initiatory moments: the initiation of the left column of the Reason of Hermes, and the right column of Jesus Christ's Love and Mercy.'

Chapter 29. About subtlety and coarseness. How to unite the two Traditions, the Hermetic and the Christian ones

13th June 1987, Kiev, hotel 'Slavutich', room No. 605, 10:00

Kasyan: 'Subtlety is an immersion in the depths of one's essence. Rudeness is continuous sliding on the surface of one's emotions and passions, excessive care for satisfying the bodily needs.

G constantly reminds me that my rudeness is my main obstacle on the path to God, but still I cannot trace and understand how it manifests itself through me.

In the East, immersion in the depths of one's soul is achieved through various meditation practices, special breathing exercises, and the like. It is difficult for a European to immerse in the deep spheres of himself according to the Eastern method, it is easier for him to do this through the practice of Christianity, that is to live according to the commandments of the Lord Jesus Christ, repenting his sins, praying to the Lord and the Most Holy Theotokos. But this practice requires a courage that is difficult to find nowadays.

There are various methods of immersion in man's subtle vehicles in different traditions. Gurdjieff e.g. gave the technique of self-observation, designed to recognize one's essence and immerse oneself in its depths, while living in the very midst of modern life. But this technique does not transform the deposits of man's mental, inner 'lead', which augments as the result of the growth of man's bad karma, into spiritual gold. Therefore, only a few people who have already reached a high spiritual level can use the technique of self-observation to immerse themselves in their essence. And if e.g. the disciples of the School, who know little about the Spirit yet, instead of performing the practices of awakening, practice the Gurdjieff technique of self-observation, then they will immerse themselves not in their essence, but in their own false personality, which grows fast having consumed the energy of the School. And instead of the growth of Cinderella, that is man's essence, the Stepmother that is the false personality will grow with her daughters, Self Esteem, Pride and Vanity. The reason for this undesirable, malevolent growth is that there is not even the idea of striving for union with the Lord in the teachings of Gurdjieff while our essence was created by God. Gurdjieff demanded that his disciples would 're-member themselves', while growth of essence and enlightenment come precisely when the disciple begins to remember the Lord and to converse with Him, to receive grace and love from Him through his purified and open spiritual heart. Therefore the teaching of Christian ascetics instructs to always remember the Lord, through prayer to Him and repentance to Him for their sins.

The alchemical School of the Ship of Fools teaches the disciple the practices of awakening.

The disciple must undergo, guided by the Master, a long process of melting and refining of his soul and spirit in various alchemical retorts of the School until the so called celestial androgyne is smelted from the disciple's uroboros. The celestial androgyne must then successfully pass the stages of Albedo, Citrinitas and Rubedo, so that one day, having accumulated the proper amount of spiritual gold inside him, he can find contact with the Creator of the Universe and the highest love.

Modern man, in order to unite with the Lord, should learn how to follow the Christian Way, using for this the elements of the Hermetic tradition. To unite the path of the hero and the path of humility, repentance and love for one's neighbour; to fuse the hermetic practices and the practices of the Christian path of salvation. It can also be called the path along the central channel of the Sephirot tree.

It comprises the practices of awakening and life according to the commandments of Christ, cultivating virtues, performing works of mercy and repenting of sins. Then the help of the Lord will come from the higher worlds, without which we will never ascend to the Kingdom of Heaven.

Chapter 30. About character building. How to obtain the subtle perception of the world. It is important to immerse in the depths of your Spirit every day. On the need to build a path of ascending. Separation of the subtle from the coarse

Sufis try to refine their perception of the world, reach out with a feather of the soul's wing to other worlds and their higher Self.

Refining however should go in parallel with character building, which is possible only in a special alchemical School. Character building includes the melting of raw, weak spots in the disciple's soul and his astral body with the help of the cosmic Ray.

The melting of raw, weak spots in the disciple's soul and his astral body and their refining takes place during the teaching situations under the guidance of a Master. If the raw spots of the soul are not melted, they constantly distort the disciple's vision, create an atmosphere of scepticism and disbelief in the spiritual path. The disciple gradually ceases to fit into the openwork atmosphere of the Ship of Fools. Damp places are like marshes in a disciple's soul, where faggots, mermen and all kinds of evil spirits live, which are always against the path of spiritual development. And when the disciple's soul and astral body have been melted to the necessary extent, or with other words, his inner marshes have been dried up and thus the habitat for all evil spirits is no more there, then his rudeness will be replaced by a subtle perception of the world, and he will feel the wind of spiritual freedom.

Kasyan: 'In our times it is very easy for a disciple to slide down to the surface of his being and thinking, to the basic needs of his body and personality, and his soul will imperceptibly fall asleep, having become identified with them and with worldly vanity. Therefore, a disciple should immerse himself in the depths of his Spirit every day, again and again in search of the spiritual pearls. Every day he must try to move his 'centre of gravity' from the coarse spheres of himself, that is from his instinctive centre, to the subtle spheres of his spiritual heart with the help of will power and super-effort. Then his essence will wake up and aspire to the Lord.

Master G: 'Immersion in the hyperphysical spheres, through the gathering little by little throughout the earth of the scattered grains of various teachings, is our primary task. For we must select the most effective practices from different spiritual traditions existing on the planet. This is necessary for building the Path of Enlightenment in our School. Then you, Kasyan, should synthesize the collected knowledge and let it germinate inside you. That is, try for yourself how it works, and only then share the assimilated knowledge with your fellow-disciples.

For the building of a spiritual path with the stress on self-development, it is best to use a synthesis of Indian and Western traditions of climbing to heaven. If you remember, we met in Odessa at the house of our common friend George, and it was Sri Yukteswar himself who sent you there. This means that I am well acquainted with the Kriya spiritual tradition and its Masters know me. And a few years later, in your conscious dreams, you already took the disciples of one of my astral schools to Mahavatar Babaji to study Kriya Yoga. This technique was created for a high-speed climb to the higher worlds. It effectively transforms our soul, physical and astral body, preparing it for the perception of higher spiritual vibrations. But Kriya Yoga alone is not enough for the crew and passengers of the Argonauts' Ship, it is necessary to combine it with other School works.

14th June 1987 Kiev, Palace of Culture of Korolev

After the 'Arsenal's rehearsal, G, looking at me sternly, said: 'There is something in you that always dodges blows when communicating with me, with other people, with Panicovsky, with Gouri-Bitumen. Those blows are a kind of correctional comments on my part and that of other disciples. You live in yourself, as if you don't need anyone. But indifference to the people around you is exactly rudeness, tactlessness, loutish behaviour.

The fact that you treat Panicovsky as a petty person, as a bore, as a continuously bilious creature, shows your fear of his insight in you. He personalizes your negative qualities, your flaws. Panicovsky sees all your weaknesses as clearly as you see his flaws. Through him many powers interact with us, millions of people stand behind him.

You cannot work with people on the tram because they will be leaving soon. Instead, you can work with just one Panicovsky, because he is strongly associated with all horizontal people. And you do not want to help your essence grow through communication with him. It's not in vain that you are invited to communicate with him, to establish feedback.

To start working more intensively on awakening your essence means communicating with Panicovsky. You however cannot establish feedback with him, because you do not understand that the growth of your essence depends on establishing contact with him. Be sure that there is a direct connection between these processes. Panicovsky sees clearly your false personality and precisely lays his finger on its manifestations. Yes, he has many flaws, but you got stuck on them, instead of paying attention to yours.

Rudeness is indifference to people, cold, causticity, while refinement is delicacy and politeness in relations with people, taking into account their interests. Caring for your neighbour, sensitivity towards him is your refinement, the sign of growth of your essence. Hermes Trismegistus said: 'Separate the subtle from the coarse.' Separating your essence from your kundabuffer, false personality and uroboros is exactly the separation of the subtle from the coarse. To do this, a disciple must perform the practices of awakening, follow the commandments of Christ, cultivate virtues and do the works of mercy. But this is still an impossible task for you.'

Chapter 31. How not to waste the current incarnation? On the need for essential communication

G said: 'It is only man's essence that can grow spiritually. The rest of man's inner composition belongs to his personality-haulm, and the haulm dies off along with the physical body. Then there is only man's essence left, but no one in general wants to work upon one's essence. Therefore, man's essence does not grow, incarnation after incarnation, remaining eternally infantile.

Shame to see the trains of wasted incarnations, senselessly disappearing in nothingness. For an incarnation is given to a person so that he uses its time for the growth of his essence, and not for bodily pleasures. For we are immortal spiritual beings temporarily incarnated in a mortal body.

So, if you want to work upon your essence, then perform the practices of awakening and at the same time study Panicovsky, in detail, carefully, then you will never feel offended by him.

Because you will be able to see what kind of alchemical reactions occur in the 'test tubes' of each disciple, you will understand why older disciples never take offense at younger ones. Because they see and know what mechanisms work inside the younger ones, and why they sometimes explode. If you want to grow spiritually, then you need to learn to master this insight at least for Panicovsky. It has no sense for you to wait for him to change, or for you to change. You must act right now.

You cannot hold a passive position: 'Let Panicovsky grow by himself, like a tree, and I will wait on the side-lines until he begins to understand and to consider me.' You have to work with him now. After all, you are not given a task to get in touch with an adept of the dark current, you would have immediately built a huge palisade around you.

There are many newcomers in the School whom you do not accept inwardly, Panicovsky including. You are very polite to him, but this politeness is only at the level of words, while inwardly you do not accept him, you do not give him room in your inner world. You have barricaded yourself from him so that even when you are together all the time, your inner worlds belong to different dimensions. Panicovsky is a rather refined person, I still did not reveal his inner worlds to you both.'

While I listened to G's admonition my kundabuffer was shrilly creaking. G added: 'I cannot order you to understand and accept Panicovsky and communicate with him sincerely, I can only call on you for this. You can deftly pretend that you supposedly understood him, but your atmosphere betrays you. Panicovsky is very keen on everyday and social trifles that you do not even notice, but he cannot understand global things, such as e.g. the mission of our School. While you think that he is aware of it and demand from him to be respectful towards the Master of the School. However there is no room in his head for the fact that I am the head of the School. Hence, his behaviour is set accordingly. And you demand from him a respectful attitude towards me, the same attitude as yours.

Refinement is when you take into account those petty / trifles that make up the biggest part of our life.'

Chapter 32. About how important it is to love your neighbours. About a cold attitude towards people. What does 'to love' mean? It is important to warm your heart

18ᵗʰ June 1987, Kiev, hotel, 10:00

Kasyan: 'Having watched the movie 'Christ', I received a tremendous impulse which helped me to understand that people must be loved and this seemingly simple condition, is the primary one on the way to God. It is much more important than doing hundreds of different spiritual exercises or saying hundreds of prayers.

A cold attitude towards people comes from the lead in the soul, and love for people comes from the gold in the soul. We easily fall into anger towards each other, but it is very difficult to feel love for our neighbour.

Jesus Christ told his disciples: 'I give you a new commandment: Love one another. Just as I have loved you, so also must you love one another.

By this, all shall recognize that you are my disciples: if you will have love for one another.' (John 13: 34,35)

How can I love someone if I have a cold heart? It must first be melted by the flaming heart of Christ.

'But I say to you: Love your enemies. Do good to those who hate you. And pray for those who persecute and slander you.

In this way, you shall be sons of your Father, who is in heaven. He causes his sun to rise upon the good and the bad, and he causes it to rain upon the just and the unjust.

For if you love those who love you, what reward will you have? Do not even tax collectors behave this way?' (Matthew 5: 44-46)

To learn to love my fellow-disciples in the School lies miles away from me. I should learn at least to respect them.

To love does not mean a back-slapping relationship, rough permissiveness and loutish behaviour. There must be always a certain distance between you and those you love. What could be better than pure and clear love for each other?

The Way of Love is the hardest of all the spiritual ways. I am not able to love those who offend or betray me. It's easier for me to hate them. I can't even fully love the Master, not to mention Panicovsky, Bitumen and other disciples. I myself will never be able to change this. I know that in order to come to love them I need to open my spiritual heart for the Lord and let His love into it. He then will include me in His love for all people.

Then thousands of petty problems that now poison the life of everyone around me would be solved. Then the atmosphere of psychological violence, which crushes everyone like a stone slab, will not radiate from me. Until the rudeness and psychological pressure on my fellow-disciples, which maintain joyless order in the School, accompanied by melancholy and despondency, would die in me, not a single elevated being will land on my shoulder.

I must learn to live for the School, and not for myself. I must stop taking advantage of the School for the sake of my selfish interests. While my heart is cold, I cannot be sincere, sincerely pray to the Lord, everything becomes a mechanical parody, a vaudeville.

To get out of my gloomy state and start transforming my lead into gold, I need to start cultivating virtues, try to live according to the commandments of God, daily perform the practice of awakening with prayer in my heart to our Heavenly Father, the Lord Jesus Christ, the Holy Spirit, the Mother of God. Otherwise it won't be.'

Chapter 33. Prayers to the Lord

22ᵈ July 1987, Moscow, Kasyan's flat, 11:45

'Forgive me, Lord Jesus Christ, for my sins, for not observing Your commandments, for not loving my fellow-disciples of the School. Forgive me Lord that I cannot perceive the depth of my teacher, although he is always with me.

Lord Jesus Christ, grant me by Thy mercy to find love in my heart. Teach me, Lord, to live according to the commandments of the New Testament. Teach me, O Lord, Thy mercy, teach me Thy humility.

Lord, deliver me from all evil, from hatred and revenge, let me find kindness of heart. Lord, guide me on the path of truth, let me be aware of my rudeness, teach me lessons of refinement and nobility. For my eyes are blinded by the brilliance of this world, and my imperfection doesn't allow me to see clearly the gifts of heaven.

O Lord, I see how imperfect I am when I think of You, and how long is my road to You. O Lord, let me understand the ways of softening and refining my callous heart.

O Lord, save me from the evil that has penetrated into my soul and corrodes my heart. Temper my heart against insults of fellow-men, inspire me to pray to You incessantly, let me enjoy love for You in the earthly world.

G: 'Everything that we met on our way, that we absorbed into ourselves, must be immersed in the depths of our spirit, in order to set in motion all those with whom we had contact.'

Chapter 34. On the sin of adultery and how to transform karma

Kasyan: 'By committing adultery,' said G, 'you waste the energy of our School, absorb someone else's karma and load it onto the School; you sink into physiology. If you do not restrain yourself from intimate relationships, then you will never enter the realm of the universal spiritual School, but if you stop fawning on every beautiful woman, then there is still a chance. In your youth you've managed now and then to touch the elevated spiritual spheres with the wings of your soul, through performing the eastern practices of immersion in your depth. However now, having abandoned those exercises without having mastered the practices of the School, you kind of dozed off completely. You became like Siddhartha, who lost his knowledge in love for a woman, having exchanged the depths of the Spirit for the surface of social life. Always communicate with all people, but never dissolve in them, otherwise you will perish.'

G is absolutely right, because after committing adultery, I feel in myself for a long time the stupidity and karma of this lady and all her lovers. Earthliness falls on me like a snowball, I become insensitive to the ethereal School wind, and it makes me plunge into the hopeless marshlands of life. Because of this, many spiritual sprouts that Master G planted painstakingly in my soul, perish irrevocably.

In order to justify an intimate relationship with the lady of a disciple's heart in the eyes of the heavenly patrons of the School, the disciple must guide her on the path of inner development, teach her the practices of awakening and how to go through the stage of purification. But, unfortunately, not every lady we liked is going to follow the path of Enlightenment. For it is said that a beautiful apple is often rotten inside.

G says that our task is to take upon ourselves the karma of our disciples and transform it into light and purity through love in our heart. Then, learn to transform the karma of cities; rising to an even higher level to transform the karma of the country, and after that the karma of the entire globe. And only then will we have the right to go beyond the gravity of the Earth, to enter the worlds of the Lord. But we cannot do this on our own, because the city's karma will instantly squash us like a steamroller would squash a frog. This can only be done by a School that is under the protection of the mysterious divine Ray and has links to the universal spiritual Schools.

Yesterday Triangle visited the 'Tibetan dead', a Ph.D., Nika, a former disciple of G. G put a lot of effort into her upbringing, and we had to try to make friends with her. Triangle entered into an alchemical reaction with the poisonous fluid of the entire scientific layer of advanced philosophical thought, of which she is a representative. The triangular magisterium did its job: slightly changed the power lines of the house of the 'Tibetan dead' and the entire intellectual philosophizing stratum of Moscow. G said that these people constitute the gold reserve of the country's philosophical thought and we need to influence it in a homeopathic way, conducting the impulse of the alchemical Ray. Gouri-Bitumen and I were poisoned by the powerful philosophical-Ahrimanic emanations and today we suffer a lot. G commented: 'If you weren't in School, you wouldn't have pain in your legs, stomach, kidneys. And since you have to be connected to various scientific fields along the way, then your entire composition squeaks and hurts, because you take on the poison of the philosophical layer, but this is mainly because you are an ignoramus.' G has been working on various social strata for a long time with the help of those specific half-disciples, half-friends of him who are firmly rooted in one or another scientific and philosophical circle of Moscow.

After visiting the house of the 'Tibetan dead' I was sick for four days. G reassured me, saying that in order not to die from the bite of a large snake, you need to get vaccinated by the venom of a small one. 'So, somewhere in the near future, I may expect to be bitten by a large snake,' I thought mournfully, instead of rejoicing that I would not die from that bite yet to come.

Today I struggled all day long against the darkness that has rained thick upon me: performed reconsideration, said many times prayer of forgiveness about the arrogant Nika. Being in such states, I become a rude and malicious, mafia-like statue, heavy and sullen, alienated from the Ray, and it takes a lot of effort for me to recycle the lead that I once again absorbed during our visit to one or another house. G says that I have to learn how to quickly process any kind of lead into gold, but this is an ideal, and for now at least into silver.

Reconsideration of the people I met, prayers of forgiveness while attending a church service, repentance and confession rid me of heavy karma. For during this sacrament, the Lord Jesus Christ dissolves all sins with His love, which is the universal alchemical dissolver of any lead in our souls. He fills our hearts with perfect purity.

Chapter 35. In order to reach the higher worlds of the Heavenly Father, the disciple has to undergo the alchemical transformation of his soul

26th June 1987, Moscow, Fairy's flat, 10:00

Kasyan-Morose: 'For many years I couldn't wake up from some kind of delusion that prevented me from clearly realizing and accepting in my essence the fact that I am a disciple of a real School of universal initiation. I couldn't therefore accept the necessity to become deeply transformed, and in quite a short time, because otherwise I could do nothing to help the Master in building the School. For some reason, it seemed to me for a long time that it was enough for me to follow the Master and help him resolve complicated issues. Indeed in the first years G needed quite a simple assistance, which Gouri-Bitumen and I could still provide, for the School consisted of just us, the two disciples and the Master. But then everything has changed and our assisting G has to become our consent to undergo regular alchemical melting and enduring the inner pain that comes with melting. Forgiving offenses from neighbours and not-neighbours, absorbing and transforming the negatives of the new disciples into something at least more positive. And all this turned to be very difficult, almost unbearable...

For it seemed to me that it was necessary to recruit such disciples who would love and appreciate the Master for the presence of the divine impulse in him. And G recruited such disciples who did not even think that he was a spiritual Master and the captain of the Ship of the Argonauts. And Gouri-Bitumen and I had to help them to make their, at best, mental, perception of the School more spiritual through long explanations. We had to console them, take care of them and absorb their negatives and grievances and transform them.

G explained to us that there are such disciples whom he has been educating for 20 years unnoticeably to them, and who attributed their spiritual insights and success to anyone and anything, but not to the influence of G. Those were, for example, the spiritual fathers and mothers of the Moscow and Petersburg cultural and esoteric Undergrounds: Admiral, Lorik, Ali, Pooh, Duda, Mamley, Rovner, Kot, Borya Yog with his cemetery team of disciples. Admiral, the most significant figure among them in the metaphysical sense, was the only one who acknowledged G as his Master, but he would always retract his words when being in a luciferic state. There were many other, less prominent, unconscious disciples who wandered around Moscow, not being able to settle in life.

The method of upbringing that G applied to me and to Gouri-Bitumen was quite cruel: G simply placed us under the initial training and polishing by his aforementioned disciples, giving them carte blanche regarding the choice of methods. Gouri-Bitumen and I absorbed into ourselves, like sponges, the mores of the alchemical master-statues and of their entourage, where Sadosha and Mazosha, as the Admiral used to say, often manifested themselves without any restraint. Therefore were taught in the same harsh way the new generations of disciples who came to G's School, to the Ship Argo, aka Ship of Fools. For this reason, we neglected G's requirements to change the teaching methodology. It is also because we did not know any other teaching method. G spoke for a long time in allegories, parables that were unintelligible to us. At some point, G told me clearly, straightforwardly, that the spiritual universal knowledge that he brought, and which Gouri-Bitumen and I were vaguely aware of and understand, no one can perceive without training. But the method of this training, suitable for our time, does not exist yet. And therefore, the patrons of the School entrusted me with the task of creating a methodology for preparing ourselves, that is, me, Gouri-Bitumen and Sanych-Panicovsky, and the new generations of disciples for the conscious perception of this cosmic knowledge. I had to select spiritual practices of several traditions, study them, test them on myself, achieve positive results, share my knowledge and skills with fellow-disciples and support them in their work on themselves.

But, nevertheless, out of inertia and out of unwillingness to take on this responsibility, for many more years I tried to educate new disciples of the School in the style of the Moscow Underground. For this, G has been mercilessly melting me, trying to plant mercy and compassion into my consciousness, which I immediately pushed out of myself, because I considered them ineffective. Having gone through many extremely harsh situations I completely lost kindness, compassion for a neighbour and condescension to his or her weaknesses.'

Chapter 36. Why is there more demand from older disciples? About G's spiritual guidance and an open heart

Kasyan-Morose: 'Our ruthless attitude towards the new disciples or those sympathizing with the School was also caused by the fact that Gouri-Bitumen and I saw that G was very kind and condescending to their laziness and faux pas , even very serious ones, and that he justified and protected them in every possible way. While on us, Gouri and me, G entrusted the responsibility for ensuring navigation and stability of our School during storms, and was ruthlessly exacting, a hundredfold, for the smallest blunders. 'How so,' we were indignant, 'everything is at our expense!'

G replied simply: 'You are much stronger than those who are now applying to join the School, and you are the foundation on which many teaching situations for new disciples is built. At the very least, you were able to withstand the main blow of the teaching situation and not abandon the School, you are more conscious, although perhaps less gifted.

There are so many talented people, disciples that ignore the good news that I brought, and only you continue following with me, the two fools, the third power of an idiot. Why do you still stay with me?'

Gradually, Gouri and I could formulate for ourselves the answer to this rhetorical question of G: all these talented people were horizontally oriented, and their talents were also focused on praising horizontal values. And Gouri and I had vertical talents that are not required, and even more to it, are recognized as dangerous in a horizontally oriented society. We followed G everywhere, for our vertically oriented abilities and talents made it possible for us to clearly see that G is an enlightened Master, who, moreover, surpassed all other enlightened Masters known to us.

Of course, G wanted to have horizontally talented disciples who could quickly help him make the School's message known everywhere. However such disciples did not stay in his company for long and disappeared into the stream of worldly life, realizing their horizontal talents. My mystical talent on the contrary, was of no use in social life, but I valued it more than my horizontal talents. Therefore, when I recognized G, thanks to this talent of mine, as a person who has found contact with God, following G and helping him became the main goal of my life. Horizontally oriented talented people couldn't see this hidden aspect of G. Even when it was revealed to them because of one or another special occasion, they did not attach any importance to it. They managed to realize their worldly, horizontally oriented talents, and my talent was an unswerving striving for God and a desire to find His shining love in my heart.

I studied with G in order to achieve Enlightenment yet in this incarnation, because I felt the presence of the Lord's influence in him, although G never promised me anything. I needed a spiritual guide who could pave the way to heaven for me.

The School on Earth has a link to both heavenly and earthly worlds. In the earthly world the School finds people who are ready to embark on the path of inner development, and then prepares them for the perception of the heavenly world. This is the reason why the disciple must meet so many various demands. For an unprepared person cannot come in the higher worlds. In order not to burn out in the radiance of the Divine fire, the disciple should purify his soul by repentance, daily performing the practices of awakening, cultivate virtues and do works of mercy.

I tried to understand this with my mind, but it gave me almost nothing. For a deep contact with the heavenly worlds, an understanding of an open heart is required, but it comes only after receiving deep inner insights ... The disciple must firmly realize that a cold heart can neither understand nor experience anything. A person with a cold heart is like a jar of dead water. Only a kind, warm heart, striving with humility, hope and faith to fulfil the commandments of Christ, can accept God's worlds.

Chapter 37. How to warm a frozen heart? Keeping your heart clean is important for resisting the powers of evil

27th June1987, Moscow, KSB, 12:00

Kasyan: 'I began to read the Holy Gospel about the coming of the Messiah, our Lord Jesus Christ, to our sinful Earth, and noble streams in my heart revived, it became filled with warm radiance at last. For in Moscow my heart cooled down, got covered with worldly soot and dust. Having absorbed at the numerous meetings with local 'hares' their horizontal karma, it ceased to feel the source of living water.

And if the heart has cooled down, and there is not a single drop of Christ's love for men in it, then what higher worlds can we talk about? And would it be possible, with a cold heart, in which there is no mercy, no compassion, no forgiveness, to be in the School which follows the Path of love?

Man's heart is quickly polluted by word, deed, thought. And it is important to cleanse it through repentance. The righteous saint John of Kronstadt teaches: 'When you lapse into sin, immediately condemn yourself sincerely and cross yourself, saying: 'Lord! Thou nailed our sins to the cross. Nail to Thy cross this sin of mine too and have mercy on me according to Thy great mercy.' Until the last day of his life, Saint Seraphim of Sarov was still saying about himself that he was the greatest sinner on Earth. And this despite the fact that he spoke to the Most Holy Theotokos and was rewarded many times with Her appearance and Her words: 'He is of our kind.'

Inclement powers set in on us In Moscow, so we lost love and trust in each other, we became cold and uncomfortable in each other's company. When the heart cools, the forces of evil can easily crush our union, G said. To resist them, we must be together in our hearts, loving each other. Keep an eye on the purity of your heart. If the heart is clean, then life in the School goes easily, but if it is darkened by selfish passions, then the School situation with its heightened mental temperature will feel unbearable.

As soon as the heart forgets about the Lord, it immediately sinks into the hopelessness and vanity of the world. No matter what you do it all will be wrong, and there will be no end to it. For the way out of the earthly world to the worlds above is to work on yourself, that is the transformation of the lead in your soul into spiritual gold.

And if you won't work on yourself daily along the three lines, it means that you do not want to reach out your hand from the Earth towards the hand that gives you help from heaven through the Master and the School. Then the heavenly worlds will always be inaccessible for you.

If the heart is pure and not darkened by passions, then you will always know how to act in difficult situations. If the heart is darkened, then you will always be led by passions that have no idea of morality and spiritual development. And, instead of performing the practices of awakening, you will chase after your passions and endless desires. And this never turns out well, but on the contrary, ends in a dramatic crash. The pursuit of passions does not teach you anything, it is just a waste of subtle energy on bodily pleasures. Therefore, you need to sacrifice your attachment to passions and repent of them.

Chapter 38. About the rules of the spiritual schools. How to create Botticelli's Spring instead of a gloomy and dreary atmosphere?

Kasyan: 'Every spiritual school is based on certain spiritual laws, which the disciple must observe at least in part. The disciple who wishes to grow spiritually will naturally be interested in learning about those laws and observe them. It must be understood that our School cannot exist if a disciples do not observe certain rules: there is no all-permissiveness and irresponsibility, as it might seem from the outside.

Of course the Ship of Fools knows not only an atmosphere of work on oneself, but also an atmosphere of celebration, which, through communication of our essences, can fill us with boundless joy. Being absolutely serious is a pretence that does not fit into the School situation, here you need to have a sense of proportion. That is to correctly combine order and clarity, on the one hand, and Botticelli's Spring, on the other. I know very well what is clarity in work and how to organize it, but it is not clear to me how to build the atmosphere of Botticelli's Spring after that. G gives etherical initiation through the state of Botticelli's Spring and awakens souls to seek salvation.

I racked my brains for a long time to understand how he does it. Most likely, he links the situation to the energies of spiritual cosmic Schools, and a bright spiritual sun lights up in his chest. Many have already witnessed the fact that when G comes, it is as if the sun comes with him, and if he leaves, then the invisible light also goes out, and the group scatters at once. Therefore, people just sit and wait for G to come. If he is not there, there is no inner life, but sadness, boredom and a horizontal atmosphere. G brings the fire of his heart, mystical subtlety, laughter, esoteric depth, the atmosphere of the heavenly world, the impulse of love of the Heavenly Father into any dreary situation.

I can gather disciples together and rub into their heads the basic hermetic doctrines that are about the importance of going through the Albedo stage and performing the practices of awakening. But there is no Botticelli's Spring in the atmosphere, for some reason it disappears. Disciples frown and look weary. 'You bring joy to people, Fedor,' G would sarcastically comment, referring to one of the characters in Mamleev's 'Vagrants'.

Now I understand that G fought against my sour atmosphere of justice according to the Old Covenant, from which even flies were dropping.

Our task is to combine in one or another impossible manner the order and lightness, justice and forgiveness of mistakes, pitilessness to ourselves and love for our neighbour, without creating an atmosphere of communist order.

We must start right now, every day, live in this bright state, and not quarrel with each other. Order should not be confused with sadism and punishment for some mistakes, which, maybe, are not mistakes at all.

I misunderstood the codes of the School, taking for them the codes of the Moscow Ezo-Underground, in which Gouri-Bitumen and I got our situational training. I therefore automatically implanted those codes with all my power on the Ship. And if someone would resist accepting them, then I discharged my anger upon the insubordinate one because of the fear that the School would fall apart and we would be lost. Now we need to work on the feeling of this false fear in ourselves: reconsider it and repent.

We can bring joy to people only with a warm heart, striving for God. To do this, we need to cleanse ourselves of horizontal karma through repentance, reconsideration, and prayer of forgiveness.

The School follows the path of love, the path of an open heart, in which the fire of love of the Creator of the Universe for all that exists burns.

The practices of awakening, keeping the commandments of God, cultivating virtues and doing works of mercy help the soul to find contact with the Lord and feel His grace.'

Chapter 39. About alchemical situations and work with different 'selves'

28th June 1987, Moscow, Fairy's House

G: 'The School creates a lot of stress for its disciples, sets millions of new tasks that they must solve on their own, straining their will, mind, patience of the heart and, at the same time, withstanding the heightened alchemical temperature. The School and its very mode of life put its disciples in such alchemical situations where they would not remain on their feet even for a day without applying a super-effort. Critical situations force us to turn on our reserves of the power of memory, patience and physical endurance.

The inner structure of a person consists of many tens of different 'selves', which constantly contradict each other. All of them are mixed in the vessel of our body, like peas in a bag. And each 'self' freely and proudly comes on the stage of our inner theatre, takes possession of our 'loudspeaker' for about 5 minutes, and angrily defends its interests, and then disappears for a long time. And then another 'self' comes on the stage and defends just as intensely quite opposite interests. And even the most intelligent person, not to mention our woeful disciples, cannot notice this.

The task of the disciple is to alchemically fuse those contradictory selves with the working group of Arjuna and thus increase the sphere of its influence in his soul.

The working group of Arjuna is responsible for the successful advancement of the Path of Enlightenment and consists of working 'selves' who fight for the spiritual freedom of the disciple's essence and perform the practices of awakening.

The School helps disciples to educate the most dense layers of their subconscious. Every day the School sets for them new problems and tasks, because horizontal life strives to replace their desire to develop spiritually with horizontal programs every day too.

To keep his feet on the Path of spiritual development, the disciple needs to tame his inner dragon, curb his passions and abandon the horizontal aspirations of his false personality.

Every day the disciple runs the risk of drowning in the worldly quagmire and falling asleep, succumbing to the illusions of maya. And if he does not wage the inner warfare every day, then he easily can become a weak-willed puppet, obeying the dark master, that is Uncle Dyoma, the demiurge. By deception, he makes man forget about man's spiritual goal, that is reaching unity with the Creator of the Universe.'

Chapter 40. About the purpose of human incarnation. About alchemical transformation. Heavy karma interferes with following the Path of Enlightenment

Kasyan: 'While solving School problems, working on ourselves, melting and polishing our interior and soul, we thereby develop inwardly, grow. If we do not follow the Path, then the question immediately arises: 'For what reason have we been born, why did we do all this work, why did we waste the precious time of our incarnation on all sorts of nonsense?' And then the answer: 'Such an incarnation is of no use to us. It's merely impossible to sate the insatiable desire to give in to passion.'

We must not allow us to let the trains, consisting of hundreds of wagons of empty, that is spiritless incarnations, run into malicious infinity due to our inertia. Man is born to let his essence grow and therefore it is wise not to go down the same road, but to aspire to the Heavenly Father, here and now.

G used to say that schooling every and each disciple requires a specific method. However no disciple can omit work on himself and repeatedly undergoing the stage of purification. A spoon-fed disciple will never make given knowledge his own and will not grow. But the knowledge that a normally developing disciple has obtained by the sweat of his brow, by the work of his own understanding, insight will forever remain in his soul and one day will bear fruit. Thus, in the soul of a disciple, a beautiful fragrant garden of love, mercy and compassion can gradually grow. And then the coveted doors to the Heavenly Kingdom, where the Lord dwells, will open for him.

Our lack of faith in God and our neglecting the path to Him is rooted in the depths of our subconscious. We ourselves are a stumbling block on the path to the Lord: our laziness and heavy karma do not allow us to embark on the Path of enlightenment. We are used to believing with our heads, but we can only believe really with our hearts. Our body does not accept God, it reduced the needs of the soul to bodily needs and work for money. There is little piety left in us, but there is a lot of violence. And our inner all the time manifests itself in critical situations, where everyone thinks only about his own interests. Why is there so little light in us and a lot of greyness, chaos, rudeness? Why is there no love for each other?

A lot depends on what atmosphere we are in, because it instils in us odd thoughts and dreams. The atmosphere is sometimes built by the powers which are far from light, and it takes imperceptibly possession of us, and we forget about the spiritual goal like weak-willed and cowardly dolls, obeying the dark master.

How to kindle the fire of your heart, the fire of love for people, how to learn to love your enemies? They say that God is within us, but when the heart is closed, it is impossible to reach Him. How to open the door in your heart to joy and love, how to learn to pull yourself out of the swamp of your powerlessness? G used to advise: 'Keep watch over your dark double inside you who love no one, are very selfish and create an over-focus on order through violence.

To stop its growth and learn to control its manifestations, it is important to focus on the interests of your essence, which seeks to unite with the Creator of the Universe. Learn to live according to the commandments of Christ, cultivate virtues and do works of mercy.'

Chapter 41. On the subtle atmosphere, essential communication and the benefits of prayer

1st July1987, Moscow, Fairy House. Arsenal in Germany, Fairy in Adler, and the Triangular magisterium in her house

Kasyan: 'If you manage to take a fancy to a person, to become interested in him, then hundreds of problems will disappear. It is difficult for me to find a way to the heart of Lord Henry: he is quiet and reserved and he is not interested in anything, a kind of riddle to himself. G says: 'If you love him with your heart, you will easily understand what is going on in his soul. Remember the commandment of God: 'You shall love your neighbour as yourself.' Try to find his shining essence in him. Find out how he lives, what interests him. Try to help him with at least something – hear him out, share with him your heartfelt warmth.'

It seems to me that I have the talent of a storyteller, to fly up on the wings of words to the heavenly palaces, to fascinate the listeners with my story. But, apparently, this is not enough, you still need a sincere interest in the interlocutor, sensitivity, attention, subtlety.

Subtlety presupposes the ability to be cordial in conversation, to create a warm atmosphere with an alchemical temperature, to master your voice, intonation. Why does everyone want to see Admiral? Because he knows how to create an atmosphere of subtle crystal-like sophistication. He carries this in his heart, in his being.

And I again locked myself in the crypt of my ego. G says that I need to focus on the remaining 'hares' and send them all the waves of care and love. In St. Petersburg those are Undi, Raek, Bandarlog-couple, Florisel. In Moscow - Dolgova, Vika, Kukusha, Matroskin, Chera, Karev-couple, Fairy, Gouri-Bitumen. In Chisinau, these are Dzhus-couple, Vera Pavlovna, Shtirlits-couple and others. 'Set yourself the task of trying to take a fancy to these people, to take care of them. Next to it you need to put together pieces of your profound but fragmented spiritual knowledge, and to create a synthesis of it. This synthesis can help many disciples to advance along the Path.

If you say the Jesus Prayer during hard physical work, then time flies happily and unnoticeably. As if it wasn't work, but prayer. Then the outside world does not draw your attention into the endless cold variety, and the heart is warmed with love for the Lord.

You need to be able to play with a person, as if with a little kitten, and then it becomes fun for him. And if you do not learn to play with people, you will never be able to master an easy-going communication.

First of all, you need to get rid of your selfishness, cease laying claims on others, learn to restrain negative emotions and try to preserve the fragile School atmosphere.

To learn from the spiritual Master of the word, you must hear his voice live, see how he creates an atmosphere, feel his cordiality. It is impossible to learn this from books. Books give you information, while the Master conveys the atmosphere of his states, through which he has contact with God. Just information about them is lifeless and resembles a graveyard of ideas.'

G: 'The magical atmosphere of the Ship of Fools gives strength and inspiration to disciples to work on themselves, kindles fire in their hearts. Everything around is filled with bright colours, and sleeping souls awaken, joyfully spreading their wings amidst the everyday life.

Kupavna, Fairy's house and KSB are the three places of power of the Etheric School Ray in Moscow. In Kupavna there is a temple in the hyperphysical dimension, access to which is guarded by the guards of the threshold, who are very frightening. When you run into them, you tremble with fear, but your task is to find a common language with them, for without this you cannot go to the crystal temple on the astral plane.

If you do not overcome your alienation from fellow-disciples and your inner coldness, you will find yourself after your death in the lower worlds. It is good that horror films make you remember about the world of darkness and nightmares, where there is no possibility for spiritual growth. This will always make you remember about the need for purification, about climbing to the higher worlds and about the need of humility before the Lord.'

Kasyan: 'Looking at Master G, I sometimes see how members of different Egregors from the higher worlds communicate with us through him. G is a kind of underwater entrance to egregorial space, to the worlds of the Lord, to the mysterious cave of Aladdin. But the door is always closed to the rude disciple.

There is no elasticity and dryness in the left half of my astral body, it is full of dampness and infernality, it is coarse, violent and contradictory in itself. And therefore, its marshlands where hags, frights, faggots and mermen, which are always aggressive towards spiritual development, live, will have to be dried out and melted.

Our Triangle, which, according to Master G, is the core of the School, is constantly followed by the spiritual egregorial powers of the advanced humanity of the Orion Ring. They come into contact with us, directly or through signs, and support our striving to find and reveal our highest Self.

Chapter 42. How not to become demagnetized in a new place. How to behave on the front line. How to become an experienced helmsman

G: 'You are often in the field of action of a strong spiritual factor, that is your Master, but if you have a wrong attitude towards him, that is, if you do not accept him in your heart and criticize him, then he cannot help you.'

Indeed, I often criticized G to myself for his minor mistakes and shortcomings. To this G said that he merely consists of hundreds of mistakes and shortcomings, but, nevertheless, the Lord communicates with him, and not with us. This means, I thought, that there is, besides the shortcomings, a huge part of G's soul for which the Lord loves him and entrusts him to carry His message to the world, while Gouri-Bitumen and I have almost nothing else but shortcomings and criticism. And our focusing on the Master's shortcomings comes from our wish to justify our own shortcomings and escape suffering caused by the alchemical melting.

A strong spiritual factor is the influence of higher powers and Egregors, standing behind the School Ray, which G conveys to the world. Therefore sharing this influence with the world should not be violent or rude, but gentle, light and appealing.

When I come to a new place, its atmosphere quickly absorbs and dissolves me, and I become a henchman of those dark spirits that inhabit it. But if I manage to overcome them with the help of the Jesus Prayer, then a small miracle occurs and a new solid alloy appears in me. It allows me to muster my strength and move further along the Path of salvation.

Master G often used to say to us: 'At the School you are on the frontline, that is, in an inner war with yourself and the infernal powers that are trying to lead you astray. And you behave as if you are at the dacha, while you need to overcome your inertia and start seriously working on yourself. It is you who must grow spiritually from yourself while the School creates the atmosphere which sustains your growth. Dozens of beings of a higher-order are simultaneously working on you, while you neglect their aid.

Gentlemen, you have overeaten and become boorish. You consider elevated gifts from above as a kind of well-earned daily ration. You take offense at every gossip and slander, but for us any gossip is a sign of the correctness of our Path. You need to work under any circumstances, on yourself, on the elements, on the environment. On a high-speed route there is no time to wait, you must always be attentive and sensitive, develop alertness. Then you will move upwards in the most difficult conditions, in the most musty atmosphere and will be able to support other disciples. And for this you should perform the practices of awakening, repent your sins, do works of mercy and cultivate virtues. You need to recollect your courage in order to follow the commandments of Christ.'

Chapter 43. A person's inner spiritual world is his true treasure. About the fragility of the world. About the two main commandments of Jesus Christ

2^d July 1987, Kupavna. G, Ifrit, Bitumen, Morose

G: 'If a person has an inner spiritual world, then this is his main treasure. The outer world is always outside of us and does not belong to us, while the inner world is always in our possession. A worldly person does not see the living world inside himself, because he is focused entirely outside. The Gospel teaches us to enter the inner world through the kindness of the heart, the meekness of the soul. When you go into the outside world, the cold penetrates into the heart, and only after going through the cleansing by confession in church, can you feel kindness in the heart, sincerity, love for your neighbour, be attentive and sensitive. We need to learn, while working in the outer world, to preserve kindness of the heart and inner depth. An indispensable part of work on preservation is alchemical cleansing of our inner and practices of awakening.'

G says that our theoretical studying of hermetic knowledge, without making our hearts warm, is even harmful. It can substantially chill our hearts. We must be able to look for depth in the simplicity of every day, to reveal the inner world, then the angels will be able to build a nest in the simplicity of our heart.

Tonight the wind picked up enormous strength and almost blew the roofs off the houses. It was G who sent the impulse of the Ray to the natural elements in order to fill them with the spiritual energies. I looked at the sky, and suddenly I felt our Earth with all its enormous mass, rushing to no one knows where in space and my soul became restless. I suddenly realized how fragile our world is, and how easy it is to lose it.

There is no love in my chilled heart for anyone and this is bad. There is a bright sun outside, but in my soul it has gone out and does not illuminate the inner path to the Heavenly Father anymore. I am dark inside like the basement of a house. I know how to light the lamp of my soul, and at the same time I don't know.

It is not always easy and pleasant to work on myself, I do not always want to pray to the Lord, but without this I will never be cleansed of the lead in my soul. And in order to soar to the Creator of the Universe, I need to spread the wings of my essence, and remove from my neck the burden of evil works and actions, which emerged by my indulging in my dark double.

It is not known how long it is meted out for me to live here on Earth, so is it worth spending my life to achieve horizontal goals? For in the next world this will be of no use to me. Therefore, the best would be to direct my footsteps and the efforts of my soul in seeking the Lord.

'One doctor of the law asked Jesus Christ,' continued G. 'Teacher, which is the great commandment of the law?'

Jesus said to him: 'You shall love the Lord your God from all your heart, and with all your soul and with all your mind.'

This is the greatest and first commandment.

But the second is similar to it: 'You shall love your neighbour as yourself.'

On these two commandments the entire law depends, and also the prophets.' (Matthew 22: 36-40).

Our neighbour for us is not an abstract person, but our Schoolmate.

We live in Kupavna as if in a beautiful bowl of flowers with the bottomless sky with multi-storey clouds floating.'

Chapter 44. Morning is a great time to immerse yourself in the silence of your heart. About the inner world of Lord Henry. On the importance of essential communication. About freedom. On self-observation and one's sincerity in relation to oneself

Kasyan: 'Every morning I try through prayer to come into contact with the higher powers that help the alchemical Ray: with the Lord Jesus Christ, the Holy Spirit, the Blessed Virgin Mary, the Archangel Michael. Through prayer in combination with hermetic practices (reconsideration, kriya yoga), I can enter into the silence of my heart. This is absolutely necessary for a successful climbing towards the higher worlds. For in the depths of our spiritual heart we can every day receive the boundless Love of the Almighty.

Yesterday I managed to come into the inner world of Lord Henry, which for him is shielded, he cannot come there. This is his inner drama. G says that in this incarnation, Henry takes a break from the great work he did in his last incarnation in the 18th century. He has a hierophantic gift, but his higher origin cannot manifest itself in the world if he will have no personal interest in the Ship of the Argonauts. It is still an issue: how to stir his interest in the alchemical teaching. Once I said to him: 'Look around, next to you there is a magic Deck of our Ship associated with the cosmic tradition. If you will join the works on the Deck, your higher origin might conceive a wish to manifest itself into the world.' Henry got enthusiastic for a day or two, but then he drew back into his shell again. It seemed to me that he could not follow his father, Master G, because of a feeling of some kind of opposition to him. As if he wished to sail his own Ship, not that of someone else, whoever it be, but at the same time he knew that he did not have enough power for this.

When the disciples of the School manage to get into essential contact with each other, the atmosphere instantly becomes deep, vibrating. And something elevated and beautiful begins to sparkle in the atmosphere.

Freedom for a disciple does not mean all-permissiveness and giving in to every whim. Freedom for a disciple means his free choice to follow the path of spiritual development. This choice imposes additional constraints on him, from the point of view of those who are committed to the pursuing of the horizontal programs during their incarnation. The Argonaut, who has embarked on the Path of Enlightenment, must, on the contrary, sacrifice his attachment to passions and horizontal values. He must also work on the transformation of his soul by performing the practices of awakening and enduring manly the alchemical melting.

Freedom must be understood as a conscious choice, with which a disciple becomes responsible for the decision he made, following actions and their consequences.

There is also spiritual freedom, to which all those who follow the Path of Enlightenment strive. This is freedom from forty-eight laws of the material world of the Earth, which fetter our soul. When we gain spiritual freedom, we open our spiritual heart and begin to feel love for the whole world, for all people, for the entire Universe. We begin to feel the light of the Divine love in our spiritual heart. And this gives us spiritual freedom, not physical. Our spirit flies in the higher worlds and dimensions, we begin to communicate with advanced humanity and spiritual Masters, angels and light spirits. And if we climb higher along the Golden Ladder, we can even communicate with the Lord.

To achieve spiritual freedom, a disciple should perform the practices of awakening, repeatedly undergo the stage of purification, and withstand alchemical melting. He must have the courage to follow the commandments of Christ, cultivate virtues, and do works of mercy.

G: 'You become sincere with yourself only when you descend into your inner hell. Here is one of the exercises on sincerity with regards to your spiritual growth. You set a proper goal for yourself, then you turn on the chronometer and begin to work on achieving this goal. You will see immediately how many factors inside you hinder the fulfilment of the set task. You will see how many of your subpersonalities strongly resist when performing practices of purification and awakening, these are reconsideration, repentance, Taoist exercises and Kriya yoga. You will observe how fear, boredom, anxiety and despondency seize you and some vile voice inside you mutters that you will not achieve any Enlightenment. And many more obstacles of this kind will arise on your spiritual Path. Just do not justify yourself by a thought that the outside world exerts strong pressure on you and does not allow you to follow the spiritual Path.

Always remember that resistance in the outside world is inextricably linked to resistance inside you. As soon as you overcome the resistance inside, then it will immediately disappears in the outside world too.'

Chapter 45. Life is like a refined chess game. How to strengthen Arjuna's Working Group. A pure soul is a young girl. How to get rid of gloominess. On the benefits of a diary of inner states

1st October 1987, Suburban train Moscow - Kupavna

G: 'Life is very similar to a complex chess game in which a person tries to become converted from a pawn to a higher chess piece, like e.g. bishop or knight. He is haunted by bad luck and besides all the forty-eight laws of earthly life prevent him from reaching the coveted position. He should manage to cross the chess-board that is life without being eaten by either a blonde beauty, or gold, or power, or illness, or a dull lazy sleep of hopelessness. Life is a subtle game, unless we are carried away by the sirens on the chess field and if we are able to not identify ourselves with our feelings and the blows of fate. But, as soon as we get stuck in one or another experience or event - that's it, the game stops completely, a bitter everyday routine comes instead, where there is no place for God, romanticism, flights of the soul. Therefore, you need to pull yourself out of the swamp in time with the help of reconsideration and practices of awakening; root out from yourself the false mind settings with their help too.'

G: 'In a dream, we have less control of our Self than when we are awake. In a dream, we completely surrender to the waves of the Great Astral and quickly forget that we have our own life, that we have a goal, that we need to act in accordance to it, we forget about God. While on Earth, we have more opportunity to focus our Self and, having recollected our strength, aspire to the higher worlds. Having gained our Self on Earth, sooner or later we will be able to climb up to heights that are still more elevated than those from which we fell, because of having not our own, developed Self. Imagine that there is a huge cotton field inside you and you can work it only through chess, and if you won't process it before the end of your life, you will die with that cotton field, and it will be taken away from you.

The search for the right state is not a search for a cool, bold experience, it is a search for the right state of action, both outward and inward. It doesn't matter what state we are in - good or not so nice, the main thing is to work well together and complete the assigned tasks, regardless of our moods. It is necessary to develop a working group of our 'selves', it is only this group that has initiative on the Path of Enlightenment and can be relied on. Only this group is able to fight for the spiritual freedom of our essence, daily performing spiritual practices and repeatedly undergoing the Albedo stage. The more the disciple raises the vertical being, the stronger the working group of Arjuna becomes. Strengthening your working group requires an effort of will and self-discipline. Don't let horizontal subpersonalities take over in the soul's realm.

How wonderful is a short-term admiration of an elegant girl who is similar to our soul, pure, luminous, joyful. Our soul, woven of subtle substances, descended from the higher worlds and is supposed to be bathed in the beauty of still renewing nature.

It is still difficult for me to get used to the fact that Master G can play a trick on my excessive seriousness at any second. In response to his words I take umbrage at him and fly into a tantrum. 'Your gloominess,' says G, 'arises from your niggling.'

Because of vain pettiness, we forgot about the main thing, about the purpose of our being at the School. In this situation, the moment will inevitably come when not a drop of light and joy will remain in the soul. We stopped cleaning our Augean stables, and now our karma has caught us. We urgently need to address this issue: to reconsider our negatives that is to regain our energy from our dark double and to confess our sins to the priest.

Quite often, Master G asks us tricky questions in order to kick us out of the state of dull aloofness and switch our attention to a working state. And when, due to pollution of our soul, we do not get the message, he repeats his favourite saying: 'He who has ears, let him hear; he who has eyes, let him see.'

'Another sense in describing your inner states in your diaries,' says G, 'is that you can monitor your inner growth. E.g. a year later you can see whether anything has changed in you, or do you still make the same mistakes, get into the same problems. Self-observation allows you to expose the false values and mechanical patterns of your behaviour that lead you away from the Path of Enlightenment into horizontal life. With the help of reconsideration you can replace your worldly mind settings with the spiritual ones and thereby strengthen your striving towards the Lord.'

Chapter 46. How to obtain subtlety of perception? Repentance frees the disciple from his karmic burden

7th July 1987, Kupavna

Kasyan-Morose: 'Whether I read the Gospel, meditate, play chess, every time I run into my barrier, that is in an untransformed lump of darkness and chaos, which bars the way for me to the higher worlds. I cannot find a common language with Panicovsky just because of the lack of subtlety in my actions. If I go through the stage of purification and transform myself with the help of the practices of awakening, learn to endure pain of alchemical melting, then I will be able to achieve subtlety in chess, backgammon, poetry, painting, in word and intonation. Then I will be able to achieve subtlety in metaphysics, where I cannot advance since long ago. And in order to intonate like Admiral, one must first get rid of false intonations. It is impossible to learn the subtle matter by one's coarse chaos, it is impossible to climb up to the higher worlds without transforming oneself and clearing one's heart and soul from heavy karma. Rough perception cannot grasp the subtleties of the worlds of light. It's like trying to measure the thickness of a hair with an ordinary ruler. One has to work on refining one's coarse perception, this might be the most important notion to grasp.

We learn to convey the atmosphere of our Ship of Fools, the atmosphere of subtle states through word and intonation. Master G educates us in a subtle and delicate manner, but often, because of our rudeness, we do not hear him.

When the disciple's energy is accumulated in the instinctive centre, he loses the ability to perceive the inspiration coming from the Master. The disciple can feel the sublime vibrations of the cosmic Ray and create a sonorous, inspiring atmosphere for the joy of himself and the School environment only when being focused on his higher centres.

Recently, I finally managed to find in myself that area of rudeness that prevented me from successfully advancing in the alchemical space of the Ship. The question arose: how can I break this lump of darkness and chaos, located on the left side of my body at the level of the physical heart? After all, it tightly blocked the way to Enlightenment.

During the reconsideration-exercise, it became clear to me that the soul was polluted because of my pursuit of bodily pleasures and from communication with rude people. I would have had to go to church, confess and receive communion in order to get rid of my heavy karma, but I put off repentance for later, hoping that my heavy karma would dissipate by itself in the company of the Master.

Chapter 47. How to enter the magic space of chess. About the Albedo stage

Master G says that chess saves him from all the troubles of life, they transform the rough atmosphere of the hotels, save him from chaos in the subway, deflect , save(? Hexes), protect him from a reverse magical blow, and help change some situations. G is an enlightened Master who has found in his heart the love of the Heavenly Father; he succeeds in whatever he undertakes. But when I try to use chess like G it deprives me of my strength and energy.

G explained to me: 'To enter the magic space of chess, one must imagine that the chess pieces come to life and slowly wander around the field, quietly talking with each other. Invite the queen to a ballroom dance first having asked permission from the king; strike up a conversation with white and black bishops; talk to pawns - ordinary soldiers and ride across the chessboard with the knight charging the tower. Thus you can discover an inner chess kingdom full of wonders.'

Since I am a rude and insufficiently alchemically-melted disciple, I didn't succeed with chess, I couldn't change myself through this game. I played chess thousands of times, but the rudeness remained in me, not allowing my essence to open up to magic and inspiration. Apparently, it was necessary to go through the alchemical stage of purification first, and only then start with chess, backgammon and other transformational games.

But when I began with alchemical cleansing, it turned out to be so time-consuming that there was no opportunity to play chess and enter its magical world. However it turned out not to be necessary for me, as performing regularly reconsideration-exercise and thus regaining the lost energy, I was able to restore the integrity and elasticity of my etheric cocoon. I thus gained the strength to struggle against my passions and also purify my soul through repentance and confession to the priest and praying while standing in church for renunciation of demons, of the dark double which lurks behind every negative manifestation of man and thus steals precious energy of man's essence. In addition, I regularly transformed my sexual energy using Taoist sublimation techniques and stored it in the lower alchemical cauldron, or Dantian.

Chapter 48. About the four Card Kingdoms

8th July 1987 Kupavna

To understand the meaning of cards, you need to penetrate into the four magical card kingdoms, where there are the kings, queens, knights, pages and servants in the form of small cards. And the Joker is a secret spiritual teacher who descended from Heaven.
There are four card kingdoms in the skies that constantly interact with each other:

The Kingdom of Spades
This kingdom is ruled by the king and queen of spades. This kingdom is located on a plain, its cities have towers and Gothic-like cathedrals. This is the kingdom of the knights of the sword. The knights of this kingdom are trying to reach heaven following the path of alchemical wisdom. The symbol of this kingdom is the owl. The knights of this kingdom organize alchemical tournaments. This kingdom is ruled by the Joker, the messenger of Heaven. He has a disciple, Faust, who tries to find spiritual wisdom. To this end, he is engaged in spiritual alchemy under the guidance of Joker. Faust is hindered by his own Mephistopheles, his dark double, who either speaks through Faust's mouth, or separates himself from Faust, materializing into a bat. Mephistopheles entertains knights and ladies at night with tales of immortality in the kingdom of the Snow Queen. He tries to lead them away from the Path of Light into the realm of cold and darkness. While the Joker possesses the secrets of various initiations of Light.

The Kingdom of Clubs
It is located in a mountainous area in an impregnable fortress. This is the mystical kingdom of the knights of the chalice, the knights of the Grail. They try to achieve im-

mortality by following the path of perceiving the Divine wisdom. This kingdom is led by the Joker too, and as a sign of this, the king wears a Joker's hat on his head. The influence of the Sixth Arcanum is strong in this kingdom, that is the choice between the heavenly, wise lady and an earthly beautiful lady, enchanting with her beauty. The knights of this kingdom walk with the ladies in the gardens along diverging paths, discussing the mysteries of love, the mysteries of the alchemical fusion of masculine and feminine origins. The knights of the cross hunt the firebird of immortality. The stellar Joker, disguised as a court jester, narrates to the queen in her secret chambers about the mystical combination of stars in the sky and the secrets of a woman's heart. The knights of this kingdom gather together regularly at the Round Table of King Arthur.

The Kingdom of Hearts.
This mystical kingdom is located on the ocean coast, it masters the elements of water and air, and it has its own fleet. Its emblem is the mystical gryphon - the guardian of the threshold on the way to immortality. This kingdom seeks Enlightenment, following the path of beauty and aesthetics and is patronized by Egregor Bagrada. The ladies of this kingdom are elegantly dressed, enchanting with their beauty the knights who know the subtleties of the female soul. The Kingdom of Hearts studies the mysteries of the androgyny, the fusion of masculine and feminine origins. Its knights and ladies are looking for the flowers growing on the tree of knowledge.

The Kingdom of Diamonds
This kingdom is located in a mountainous area and is an impregnable fortress with high thick walls. It is a stronghold of purity and chastity. The knights of the spear live there. On their shields the lion, a symbol of the sun, open heart and kindness is depicted. The entrance to the kingdom of the Cross and the Rose is guarded by a huge lion. The knights of this kingdom worship the Virgin Mary, per-

forming countless deeds in her honour. The ladies of this kingdom are dressed simply and nobly, their faces reveal beauty and meekness, they hold high spiritual ideals. The knights of this Kingdom undertake long-lasting missions for the spreading of Christian ideals. This is where the true knightly-ascetic character is built.

Only the Joker knows that the Kingdom of Heaven can be reached by the joint efforts of the Four Kingdoms.

Chapter 49. On how to transform one's horizontal being into a ritual, dedicated to God. It is important not to lose feedback with each other. How to withstand the Heavenly Fire. What is the right way to partake of the Gospel

19th July 1987, Kupavna

G: 'The crew of the Alchemical Ship will have to make an effort to transform horizontal being into ritual being. All our travels should become a ritual, which conveys an impulse of inspiration, then the concerts of 'Arsenal' will become inspirational too.

How to do it? If we in our hearts pray every moment and thus do all our works with prayer, then our horizontal being can turn into a ritual. We must devote all our works to the Lord, even washing the dishes. Washing the dishes for the Lord is not an easy task, it is an event, more than just a prayer. The more of your inner centres participate in prayer, the faster you rise and purify your soul. Even an ordinary bike ride can turn into a ritual with the help of prayer. Our task is to devote all our works to God in love. And if all our actions are filled with the current of the New Testament, the current of love of our essence for the Lord, this will make our being an initiatory one. So far, only you and Gouri plucked up courage to follow me.

If while in this physical life we carry together the proclamation of the cosmic Ray, then after the death of our bodies, our union will not fall asunder and we will continue serving this proclamation. You must always be the conductors of the mysterious Ray, the wind of which always blows into your sails. Your problem is that you don't always set them up. We must here find feedback with each other in all situations, then we will not be lost even after death and will work in resonance.

If we do not lose feedback with each other even in Fairy's space and survive there as a whole, then we can come to the eye of the needle, through which the passage to the Kingdom of Heaven leads. Following the commandment of Jesus Christ: 'Love one another' (John:13:34), we can devote this incarnation to God, and our whole being will change.

And if we only drink, eat and relax, without remembering the Spirit, our life will quickly degenerate into another empty incarnation.

There is a mysterious knightly order in the Universe that serves the fire above the Grail. It is somehow related to the Parsi belt, which also serves the Heavenly Fire. And Ancient Egypt is associated with the Parsi belt and the Moscow region.

You have to strengthen your vertical being, otherwise, when climbing up to the higher worlds, the soul will burn in the fire of the Lord, like the wings of a butterfly burn in the flame of a candle. But having got rid of heavy karma and having transformed yourself with the help of the practices of awakening, you can withstand the cosmic power of the Heavenly Fire.

They say that Raphael and Leonardo Da Vinci were in one of their past incarnations the apostles of Christ. It is important to act as if God looks through us into the human world. I advise you to look at the paintings of the great masters, depicting scenes from the Gospel. There is something more concealed behind the image there. When you will become imbued with the Gospel and read it in Old Church Slavonic and Russian, there will be revealed more to you than you find in it now.

You must penetrate into the initiatory traditions of the Ring of Orion with all your being, feel them and learn them in order to become a citizen of the Universe and one day reach your Higher Self, filled with love for the Creator of the Universe.'

Chapter 50. Comments on the film 'Cyrano'

7th October 1993 Dordrecht, Satya's ashram. Comments on the film "Cyrano"

G: 'The Initiate is the great Anon and he always manifests himself anonymously. The alchemical knowledge is to be found in the novels of Hugo, in the plays of the classics of French drama. There appears always an actor instead of the Master on the stage and he performs an action, designed by the Master, in order to share a mysterious Impulse. The main characters are always the same: 'the cheap opera singer Giglio Fava' and 'the poor beautiful seamstress Giacinta'.

The Master stays behind the scenes, sharing with the actors the egregorial wind of romanticism. Being inspired by this wind Giglio Fava and Giacinta begin their improvisatorial play. They become temporarily the main characters, sharing with the spectators the wind of the Impulse. Spectators applaud their performance, everyone begins to love and respect them, they become interesting people, they are praised by blossoming life. But as soon as the great Anon leaves the actors and ceases sharing with them the impulse of the cosmic Ray of the School, they become uninteresting, common people. The same happens with any disciple of the School, should he fall out of the field of action of the School Ray. He becomes then an ordinary person, that is the one who is captured by the illusory dream of Maya and has forgotten about his spiritual nature.

The Master is always alone, his fate is always idiotic and tragic. For the successful sharing of the Impulse, the Master always acts through dummies, this is his tragic sacrifice. The apparent manifestation of the XII Arcanum, that is Sacrifice on the Path of Enlightenment...

...In reality, I do not act on you directly, but always through other disciples, through various life circumstances that change when you come into contact with the cosmic Ray. But if you want to continue to take part in the action of the Ray, you need to purify the soul with the help of reconsideration and repentance and perform the practices of awakening. Only then you can begin to learn to live according to the commandments of Christ, cultivating virtues in yourself. First the Master had to buy you out with cosmic currency, linking you to the spiritual energy of the mysterious Ray of the School, involving the Ray in this action mainly on his own energy and initiative. But after that, you should go through the stages of alchemical transformation; only then will you begin to really develop, playing various roles in the theatre of life. You learn to change your roles in life and your tactics until you fall for the sweetest piece of the Ship's pie and run away with it, like the rat Shushera... Having sank, without the support of the Ship of Fools, into the dark basements of your soul, you will enjoy the stolen pie... But you do not have the recipe for this pie, and having had gnawed the last bone, you will again return to your worthless horizontal existence... However there is nothing wrong with that either, the rat Shushera was the former best disciple of Papa Geppeto, who, due to her selfishness and neglecting the work on herself, turned from a beautiful Thumbelina into a terrible little monster...

Cyrano all the time arranges catalytic circumstances for the overfed, worthless, self-eating-like existence, introducing people into a situation of eternal paradox. He leads his actors through many alchemical distillatory cubes and continual melting, waiting for the emerging and maturation of their personal striving towards the Spirit. He gives them a chance to wake up and perfect their soul. And when they are ripe, he will inspire them to perform the long-term work on themselves with the help of the practices of awakening and cleansing.

The Teacher might accomplish some necessary work on the disciples, but it is they who must accomplish the greater part of the work on their souls on their own. No one is able to do this work for them.

An etherical proclamation is manifested through Cyrano's entire being, it is the super-consciousness which manifests itself.

The two-dimensional logical mind of ordinary humanity is not able to understand the paradoxical behaviour of the Master, it is always hostile to the manifestations of the Anons. Cyrano did not give lectures to the smug, inane bourgeois, he introduced them into the reality of the Impulse through a paradoxical situation. Cyrano directly introduced people into a situation of paradox so that their horizontal being would grow too. The young man, thanks to his purity, recognizes the Master, becoming his disciple through the initiatory intrigue. Roxane - Giacinta, whom he is madly in love with, is too beautiful to directly perceive the impulse of the Master. The Master uses therefore an indirect method: he includes in the game Christian - Giglio Fava, a young man who has become his disciple. A crude, but outwardly beautiful 'puppet', which, through his love for the stupid Roxane-Giacinta, enables them both to perceive the highest initiatory Impulse.

And on the Ship of the Argonauts the same eternally unique miracle is taking place, which could never happen at the end of the twentieth century and, nevertheless, for some reason, it happens, but few people appreciate it, because they cannot understand what's going on. We, too, try to convey the initiatory Impulse through the stalker's intrigue and improvisation, through the ethereal atmosphere, and very rarely we read lectures to laymen.

Chapter 51. About the struggle for 'a place in the sun'. On inspiration in art. 'There are no delays to visit God.' How to stop playing the role of the cheap opera singer Giglio Fava

Louis-Claude de Saint-Martin (1743-1803), French freemason, philosopher-mystic, spoke of such initiation through which the Highest Unknown is manifested. We always find ourselves in a place cut off from the rest of the world, which allows us to stress the acuteness of the initiatory moment without much hindrance. The secular world would immediately begin to lower us, imposing its outward significance on us.
Through Cyrano's love for Roxane, Vertical's love for Horizontal is manifested. In the sphere of action of the Ray, everything sprouts at the very least.

'There are no delays when visiting God.' Cyrano, through his last message to Roxane, made her understand that the play that he played in for her had come to its end, Cyrano was dying. Everything, gentlemen, is a play. Roxanne only now realized who was the real inspirer of her heart, who was the source of love in her heart, but it is too late now, the Master died. Initiation however will live forever...

Cyrano managed to captivate the Horizontal through love, subtlety, awe - this is a manifestation of the mystical initiation. In the beginning, Cyrano manifested magical initiation through fights, duels and happenings. He gave kabbalistic initiation through the speed of understanding, speed of action, speed of reaction. The hierophantic initiation combines the magical, the mystical and the kabbalistic initiations, and on their basis conveys the wind of an unknown transcendental space.

Each planet in space struggles for its existence, for its initiation, against other planets; each solar system struggles against other solar systems, reclaiming its 'place in the sun'. So the disciples will have to struggle for the spiritual freedom of their essence, for the reaching of the Kingdom of Heaven. This struggle always takes place within oneself and is aimed at curbing the dark double, refining the soul, cultivating noble qualities of the soul necessary for communication with the higher worlds. At the same time, it is important to be strict with yourself but show care and mercy to the fellow-argonauts of the Ship. Thus you can bring the laws of the New Testament into your being.
Hoffmann was inspired by the Baltic Archangel, and through Shakespeare and his writings, the Archangel of the North Sea spoke.

Don Quixote was the bearer of the wind of the Golden Ladder, the Grand Master of the Order of the Templars, while outwardly he was an absolutely crazy, cast-off old man, who drenched himself in the tales of chivalry. Now he took himself off to more glorious worlds up the Golden Ladder... People who have watched the movie about Cyrano leave without watching the credits or listening to the inspirational music. This aborts their impression of the movie, turns on the system of 'red flags' and thus through 'righteous pride' their souls fall into the lower worlds. Initiation is often conveyed through music, through the subtle spheres of the Art.

Etheric proclamation is always given through figureheads. And you, Kasyan, are exactly such a figurehead which became aware of this, you are an actor and no more.
But if you will work on yourself correctly, that is purifying your soul and performing the practices of awakening, if you will embark on the Path, then you will be no more the figurehead Giglio Fava. And one day you will be able to reach the higher worlds, and the theme of any initiatory tragedy is one and the same, that is the love of the spirit for

the chosen soul and the manifestation of the spirit through the initiatory miracle of the soul's tragic life.

Chapter 52. About the main problems arising in the creation of a close-knit team on the Ship. What is needed for establishing feedback between the Argonauts. How to link to the Hermetic Tradition

The main problems in any activity on the Ship of Fools, including the creation of its close-knit team, are:

1. Establishing an essential feedback between disciples;
2. Ability not to touch on the other's sore places;
3. Establishing feedback between disciples and the Hermetic Tradition;
4. Search for the footholds for the School
5. The disciple's self-preparation for life after death on the hyperphysical plane.
6. The disciple's self-preparation for incarnation on another planet or in another star constellation.

1. To establish an essential feedback with each other, it is important to rise to the level of the spiritual heart. This will allow you to be sincerely interested in the fellow-disciple, learn about his problems, show concern, forgetting about personal gain. Such communication helps essence to be found and gives it the opportunity to manifest itself freely.

2. The ability not to touch on each other's sore spots is a great art, disciples must learn to be very considerate with each other. However if it did not help and a conflict situation arose, you need to discuss the points of tension. Do not defend your innocence or righteousness, but show flexibility and give in, keeping in mind the primary necessity to preserve the team spirit. A disciple must be able to control his dark twin, not allowing himself to manifest

selfishly and rudely, this will preserve the subtle atmosphere of the Ray.

3. In order for the disciple to establish feedback with the Hermetic Tradition, he must imagine his whole life as a School in which the study of the Hermetic Tradition takes place. In this School, he undergoes an alchemical transformation: melting lead deposits in his soul (negatives and passions) into noble qualities.

The disciple's self-transformation methods are as follows:

- the disciple's observation of his negative manifestations and describing them in his diary;
- withstanding the melting of the raw spots of the soul under the impact of the alchemical Ray, that is acceptance of correctional comments and admonitions of the Master and other Argonauts;
- reconsideration-exercise regarding horizontal life, prayers of forgiveness and repentance of sins;
- performing prayer and contemplation practices of awakening.

4. The search for the footholds for the School includes the building of the harbours where the Ship of Fools can moor.

5. We should prepare ourselves for life on the hyperphysical plane by constantly purifying the soul and regularly performing the practice of Kriya Yoga. This will help to withstand the high-voltage energy of the higher worlds. If the soul is pure, then the guards of the threshold will allow it to come into the worlds of light. In addition, the disciple must master the technique of astral travel and lucid dreaming.

6. We face the task of preparing ourselves for life on another planet or even in another star constellation. To do this, we need to deeply immerse in the Christian tradition. Learn to live according to the commandments of Christ,

cultivate virtues in ourselves and do works of mercy. For some adepts of the Ring of Orion incarnate deliberately on the planet Earth in order to join the Christian tradition.

Almost all of the traditions of the earth encompass only planetary initiations. The Hermetic tradition, also called the Stellar Tradition, encompasses not only planetary but also all the stellar initiations. Having received the planetary initiation, the disciple can only move between the astral planes of his planet, depending on the severity of his karma. And to work in other areas of the Universe, you need to raise your level of vertical being so much that you can practically master all earthly traditions plus receive the stellar initiation of that specific area. But this is still a very, very distant project for you.

Chapter 53. On the importance of astral travel. About establishing contact with higher humanity. How the knowledge of the stellar tradition came to Earth

Many planets of the Orion Ring are inhabited by human beings of different shapes, but with the same soul structure. Also in our Solar System, the planets are inhabited by human beings on the astral plane (Venus, Mars, Jupiter's moon Io). This is knowledge that belongs to the Hermetic Tradition. But all this can be verified through personal experience. This hermetic knowledge came to us from Ancient Egypt, later it was lost, but revived in the form of the Arcana Taro.

One of our tasks is to establish feedback with the Hermetic Tradition and with other human beings living on other planets and on the astral planes. This will be possible when disciples master out-of-body travel. For example, Fairy has been engaged in astral travel for a long time and you can learn this art from her. That is, you have to learn to leave the physical body being in your astral one, and master lucid dreaming. In other words, to grow a magical body for travel. This is evidenced by the European alchemical tradition, Hindu tradition, as well as Sufism and George Gurdjieff.

We can feel the stellar Tradition through symbols, for these are symbols of the highest humanity living on other planets and in the hyperphysical space. This is a connection with higher developed human beings who are also studying the Hermetic Tradition.

When being in a pure state of mind an Argonaut can feel the energy of the higher worlds. Through tuning in to higher humanity, our souls are filled with subtle energy, a kind of spiritual oxygen necessary for the growth of our essence. Then comes joy full of grace, a feeling of inner fulfilment, inspiration, positive strength, love for people, expanded consciousness. You can see the life of the higher worlds with your inner eyes, put questions to the members of different Egregors, ask for help in your spiritual development. Without the support of advanced humanity, it is very difficult to reach your Higher Self, which is like the spiritual sun, filled with love for the Creator of the Universe.

How did the knowledge of the stellar tradition come to Russia? It came to us from ancient Egypt and Tibet, where it came from the lost Atlantis, and if you look further into the past - from Lemuria, Hyperborea. This is the stellar Tradition of the Milky Way. It is intended for all human beings who are ready for it. Many traditions relate to this, but the key is hidden and the knowledge is shared by word of mouth, through the subtle atmosphere of the alchemical Ray; it is impossible to do this through writings.

Chapter 54. About four aspects of the stellar knowledge. The disciple must be honest with himself. About the Sufi tradition. Can common people accept the Hermetic tradition?

It is necessary to create a mystical wind that will help to assimilate the stellar knowledge. And this is the mystery of the Grail, after which experience your soul may karmically touch the secrets of the Round Table of King Arthur. Part of this knowledge was possessed by the Knights of the Round Table, the other part was hidden in other sources. We are trying to combine four aspects of Universal knowledge: magical, strengthening the will; kabbalistic, developing reason; mystical, heart-opening; and hierophantic, which brings the afore mentioned aspects together. Jesus Christ brought something that was not previously included in human development, and which is associated with the spiritual heart of a person, the hierophantic aspect hidden in the mystery of the Holy Grail. There were Schools in Russia studying the Hermetic tradition, and gradually they approached the stellar traditions. Christ made it possible to understand it not only through reason and will, but through the heart, the highest human ability, cognition through feelings, the hierophantic aspect.

It is necessary to be attentive to yourself, not to deceive yourself, not to imagine and not fantasize. Fantasizing is good for the soul, but it is also important to be honest with yourself, with your essence, which is the divine spark of the Absolute. You need to see yourself without embellishment, having thrown aside your pride, vanity and feeling of self-importance.

Only then can you take on real work on yourself. Otherwise, you will see yourself through rose-coloured glasses, idealizing and deceiving yourself.

At one time, some spiritual teachers passed on the Universal tradition, but now their teachings have turned into a museum, that is there is a form, but there is no link to God. The museums are also necessary for the sake of preservation of the tradition, but even more needed is the direct sharing of it through the atmosphere with the souls seeking Enlightenment.

The question arises: are only specially trained people capable of accepting the Hermetic tradition or the common, unprepared people too?

Here the two existential opposites meet each other. Each person has a karmic history, has specific talents. For example, a mediumistic talent, which is also a very dangerous talent. The energy source might be closed, and what is the use of this talent then?

If you want to learn the Hermetic tradition, you need to start performing the practices of awakening, repeatedly undergo the stage of purification, and endure the alchemical melting. When you will become magically stabilized, that is stop feeling sorry for yourself and fall to pieces inwardly, then you can start studying it. But in order to perceive the astral plane and learn to act in it, you must master the technique of getting out of the body. You also need to open your higher centres and cleanse your soul and heart from passions.

The Monk Silouan the Athonite said:

'A soul that has come to know God learns through a long experience that if a person lives according to the commandments, at least to some extent, he feels grace inside him and has boldness in prayer. But if he would sin with just one thought and does not repent, then grace abandons him and then the soul yearns and weeps before God. Thus the soul is busy its whole life with the struggle against thoughts. But do not be discouraged by the struggle, for the Lord loves the courageous fighter.'

Chapter 55. The theme of the VIIth Arcanum: opposition of the black and white sphinxes. The theme of the XVth Arcanum: how to overcome Baphomet in yourself? Our goal is to learn how to control both sphinxes

On the card of the VIIth Arcanum, the Winner is depicted. He controls a chariot driven by white and black sphinxes. The chariot is a symbol of the physical body of the disciple, and the sphinxes symbolize bodily manifestations.

The white sphinx represents bodily virtues, namely bodily activities that lead the disciple to the light worlds of the Three-One God. These include, as taught by the Christian-Hermetic ascetics, moderation in food, clothing, comfort, sex; knowledge of the basics of herbal therapy and therapeutic exercises; avoiding crowded meetings and long conversations; regular prayers in front of icons with prostrations and kneeling, prayer and breathing practices of awakening with prayers to God the Trinity, the Mother of God, the Archangel Michael, the guardian angel and saints; mastering many professions and the ability to earn a living; charity if possible and care for those in need, giving alms.

The black sphinx represents bodily passions that carry us into the dark worlds, destroy our body and eventually make us slaves to demonic obsessions. Examples of bodily passions: gluttony, craving for luxury, drunkenness, various types of voluptuousness, debauchery, and all sorts of unnatural and shameful passions, as well as theft, sacrilege, robbery, murder. A life according to the passions is a life subordinated to the pleasing of the body, dulling the mind and making it animal-like, and preventing the disciple from looking up to God and to works of virtue.

We cannot get rid of the black sphinx and remain only with the light one, because after the fall of our Universe, the black sphinx also forms part of our inner nature.

The winner is the disciple who has learned not to get carried away and not to be identified with either the white or the black sphinx, but knows how to control the white sphinx and to prevent the manifestations of the black one. For example, if a disciple is fanatical, excessively carried away by bodily exercises, forgetting that they are only a means of coming closer to God, and not a goal, he may, unnoticeably to himself, be captured by the black sphinx. When a person advances on the path of Enlightenment, performing spiritual practices, then both sphinxes grow. But the black one grows much faster, because planet Earth is not a very bright place.

If the disciples do not perform the practices of awakening, then the horizontal vortex quickly picks them up and carries them further and further away from spiritual development, from the mysterious alchemical Ray.

In order to curb the black sphinx, disciples have to return regularly to the Albedo stage during their entire incarnation. That is to cleanse the soul of passions and negatives with the help of repentance and confession, prayer of forgiveness and the reconsideration of the horizontal life and indispensably withstand the alchemical melting.

For the sake of the alchemical transformation of the soul and the cultivation of virtues, the disciple must humbly accept the corrections of the Master and senior students regarding his shortcomings. For the black sphinx will not let him notice them.

The theme of the XVth Arcanum is touched upon here. Until you overcome the XVth Arcanum - Baphomet inside you, you will not be able to reach the stars. In the Christian tradition, all saints fight with demons, this is called 'spiritual warfare'. You have to come to know your hell, your dark double and defeat it and control it. In Arcanology, Baphomet is the guardian of planetary space: you cannot break out of the planet and rush to the stars if you have not defeated Baphomet inside you. When you experience feelings of hatred, jealousy, you immediately relate to your black sphinx, which is directly related to Baphomet. The disciple's task is to keep track of his negative states in order to transform and dissipate them later.

To do this, you need to go through the stage of purification in time, perform the practice of awakening, follow the commandments of Christ, cultivate virtues and do works of mercy.

A person is rather strongly identified with his black sphinx and is not able to track and fight his negative states on his own. Many people even have an infernal idea that their negative emotions should be discharged on people who made them feeling irritated. Thus, they strengthen their negative qualities, sooner or later negative crystallization takes place, and they become antisocial persons. It is necessary to find a third force that is capable of controlling two sphinxes, this is the help of the higher powers. Therefore, it is important to turn to Christ, the Mother of God, the Archangel Michael in heartfelt prayer, so that they protect the soul from all devilish powers.

It is necessary to pray not mechanically, but from the depths of the heart, realizing the meaning of the words of the prayer.

You need to consciously observe the manifestations of the white and black sphinx in you. The white sphinx proposes one and the same riddle to the disciple: 'How can you reach your Higher Self, how can you become one in your heart with the Divine love of the Creator of the Universe?' Having solved it, the disciple will feel that his spiritual home is not the planet Earth, and not even the solar system, but the higher spiritual worlds.

Chapter 56. About conscious and mechanical suffering. How to rebuild your life in a vertical way? About the purposeful blow of George the Victorious to the dragon

The idea of conscious suffering is associated with the restructuring of the human soul, with the construction of new axes, new molecular magnets in it. This is precisely the hermetic restructuring of the soul, the tendency of the XIVth Arcanum, which in the Hermetic tradition is called the 'harmonium mixtorum'. Conscious suffering is, first of all, working on your self-esteem. But it felt easier for any disciple to do hard physical and even psychological work than to work on his self-esteem. Each disciple's self-esteem has its own sore points, touching which excites his anger. Moreover, he feels this anger to be righteous, therefore he gives in to it completely and loses even more of his subtle energy. Disciples lose a lot of their subtle energy through the feeling of self-pity, too. E.g. if a disciple suffered greatly in his childhood, he might feel great self-pity and to take revenge for everything: a negative emotion through which his energy leaks.

Being in the School the disciple has a possibility to undergo a series of teaching situations to work on his sense of self-esteem, to defeat his dragon through conscious suffering. The disciple suffers consciously when he follows the path of spiritual development, while outside this path he suffers mechanically.

When a person faces the choice to embark on the Path of Enlightenment instead of serving his horizontal interests, he begins to experience conscious suffering because of the diminishing of horizontal riches.

When a disciple faces a choice between following the School or his horizontal aspirations, the need arises to suffer consciously. The dragon suffers, for he is very hurt and wounded, St. George the Victorious has delivered yet another blow to the dragon. This is already voluntary, conscious suffering of the disciple who accepts this blow. On the emblem depicting St. George the Victorious, the dragon symbolizes horizontal life, horizontal values, and the lance aspiration towards vertical life. The disciple's desire to develop spiritually is very painful for the dragon.

The words 'mechanical' and 'conscious' are indications, and their use is determined by what a disciple suffers for: to achieve goals in material life or in spiritual life. Does the disciple fight for his spiritual advancement or for the survival of his physical body on Earth? In both cases, it is painful.

A disciple suffers consciously when he endures psychological pain during the alchemical melting of the raw spots of his soul, when his fellow-disciple or his neighbour points out to him his shortcomings, like his attachment to sinful passions, anger, fornication, greed, deception, etc. Endure suffering when performing the practices of purification and awakening. Endure suffering and withstand temptations while trying to live the commandments of Christ, cultivating virtues, and doing works of mercy.

To suffer mechanically means to suffer from the fact that it was not possible to satisfy the disciple's passions, to acquire and amass horizontal riches.

Chapter 57. About the defence of one's pride by means of a duel. How to become a knight of the spirit and curb the dragon? On the principles of the Old and New Testaments. About sore points and how to work them out

There is earthly chivalry, which defends the horizontal interests of the state, of which those knights are subjects, as well as spiritual knighthood, which fights for the spiritual freedom of man's essence, which makes every effort for the sake of salvation of the soul and achieving unity with the Lord.

One example of the delusions of earthly chivalry is the so called 'defence of honour through the duel'. Many knights killed each other, believing that they were defending their hurt honour. In fact, it was only their self-esteem, their pride that was hurt. The knights who are trained to defend horizontal values can hardly discern the difference between honour and pride. Therefore, those knights often confused them and just wasted their life or the life of their opponent that the Lord had given to them. Most people think that the fight takes place only on the physical plane, but it is the contrary: the main battle takes place on the various planes of our soul. The knight is a master of martial arts in the fight against the black sphinx. But man can also be a knight of his black sphinx, a knight of darkness, who conveys the black winds. The knight of light does not fight against the physical body of his adversary, but against the dragon that lives in it. Peter denied Christ three times, for we are all under the dominion of the world of evil. But the knight knows how to curb the dragon, which is hidden in us and is closely related to the Kundalini. We cannot kill him, otherwise we will die, but we can transform the dragon, since there is something higher than the interests of the dragon living in us. Therefore, you can become either a Master or a zombie of your inner dragon. A person who possesses real power does not demonstrate it and does not spend it like hot water, he is always humble. It is forbidden to kill a man, for he is sacred, but it is possible to curb the dragon in him.

The old world lived according to the principles of the Old Testament: 'An eye for an eye, a tooth for a tooth.' We have a chance to become more civilized people and live in accordance with the New Testament, that is, to love our neighbour as ourselves. But everyone still lives according to the principles of the Old Testament, mired in their selfishness, pride, vanity, greed and lust for power. To transform this, you need to be very keen on observation of your negative manifestations. 'An eye for an eye' is also good, but this is the tradition of Moses, a tradition based on justice, and Moses did not say anything about immortality. The tradition of the New Testament is based on forgiveness and love, and this is necessary if you want to become immortal and rise to the stars. Pain can be transformed into a blessing if you begin to observe yourself and work through your sore points, that is, the raw spots of your soul.

To work through your sore points, you need to endure humbly the psychological pain when the Master or senior disciples correct you. To withstand psychological pain during alchemical melting, to forgive insults, not to justify yourself, not to snap back and not to feel sorry for yourself, not to store up bitterness. In addition, it is important to return to the Albedo stage over and over again and go through it, performing the practices of cleansing.

Chapter 58. About the highest honour and the experiences of the divine soul. It is important to find time for spiritual development. The Ship of Argonauts helps disciples to realize their cosmic soul. What does honesty with yourself mean

If a person wants to develop spiritually, he encounters conscious suffering that accompanies the struggle for the sake of finding his Higher Self, finding the love of the Lord.

We have well organized our physical life, procreation, but the Hermetic tradition says that we should also take sufficient time to perform the practices of awakening, to achieve unity with the Lord. Then our incarnation will not be in vain.

We are not only a physical and astral body, we also have a cosmic soul and a Higher Self, and we must manifest them and feel them. The Holy Grail is associated with the tradition of the heart, these ideas cannot be realized without support from the depths of our spiritual heart. For if you love the Lord, then you forget about pride. This is the ideal of King Arthur's Knights of the Round Table . You can help another person in the survival of his physical body, but he might also have a very strong spiritual hunger, and then your help in achieving his spiritual goals is much more important. Helping people to survive the physical body is very well developed in modern civilization. But little attention is paid to help in realizing one's cosmic soul. The Ship of Fools is doing just that.

Honesty in relation to yourself is whether you sincerely want the awakening of your cosmic soul; whether you do at least something for your spiritual development in this incarnation. For example, do Kriya Yoga every day, and not just preaching love, harmony and beauty. It is very difficult to do this, but it means finding a link between the earthly soul and the cosmic one.

Chapter 59. About stalking and hermeticism

'The whole world is a theatre.
And all women and men are actors in it.' (W. Shakespeare)

Mastering the art of stalking means the disciple's skill to hide his spiritual life from horizontal people, for ordinary life doesn't approve spiritual aspirations.

The stalker learns to be a good, versatile actor in the theatre of life. He does not identify with the horizontal life, and he knows that people are generally mediocre, unconscious actors, while he is a conscious actor, for whom life is a stage for a number of his roles. He can find a common language with any person, easily tuning in to the atmosphere of his interlocutor.

A major part of neophytes spout on their spiritual quests and thus waste their subtle energy. The inner, spiritual cup of perception should be tightly sealed.

Jesus said: 'Do not cast your pearls before swine.' (Matthew 7:6) This means that it makes no sense to share spiritual knowledge with those who do not seek it and do not appreciate it, who are not ready to receive it, as well as with those who are mired in worldly passions and do not care about the salvation of their souls.

The disciple should take pains to share with others through his atmosphere a normal human attitude, normal feelings, and give people something not through words, but through his attitude, that is in a hidden, hermetic way. So you can warm their sleeping essences by sharing with them a bit of spiritual oxygen, that is the energy from the higher cosmoses.

But do not expect respect from your neighbours and acknowledgement of your spiritual merits. You must respect yourself and you do not need respect and recognition from the chaotic life around you. If you have reached a certain level of spiritual life, then you begin to project it into your environment.

This means the awakening of the disciple's inner child, who is connected with his inner being. He returns to his essence, to his inner spiritual core, in contrast to the horizontal people who develop at the best, their personality that can only amass knowledge but cannot grow spiritually. Jesus said: 'Unless you change and become like little children, you shall not enter into the kingdom of heaven.' (Matthew 18:3)

Each race carries with it one of the aspects of the Hermetic Tradition. For example, the Black Race has received a magical Initiation, the centre of which lies at a certain place on the Black Sea coast. And the tradition of George Gurdjieff belongs to the Parsu Initiation Belt, which covers South China, Central Asia, the Caucasus, Tibet, this is the Initiation of Fire.

We belong to the White Race and we are studying its tradition. The main symbol of the Initiation of the White Race is a triangle, the flame of the fire of spiritual ascent. Jesus said: 'I have come to cast a fire upon the earth. And what should I desire, except that it may be kindled?' (Luke 12:49)

Jesus Christ incarnated on Earth two thousand years ago, He was not only the last Messiah, the Messenger, but also the One who sent, that is, God himself. The idea of the New Testament is to bring Heavenly Fire to our Earth, that is, to kindle Divine Love in the hearts of people.

But this teaching is always shared by word of mouth, it is sealed. According to the Christian tradition, our cosmos is fallen since Adam and Eve were tempted by Lucifer, and the intention of the initiation of the White Race, white is to return to paradise, but in a new state.

The essence of man must follow the path of spiritual development in the course of many incarnations and return to our Heavenly Father. One of the meanings of the letters INRI on the cross of Jesus is as follows: Igne Natura Renovatur Integra, which means: 'By fire nature is restored in purity, or pure matter is restored by spirit.' Christ was fire and through Him we find our way into another dimension, into the dimension of eternal life.

Chapter 60. The goal of spiritual wanderers is to restore the link to the Creator of the Universe. About the Hermetic Tradition. About Sufism. Universal wisdom and higher humanity

A part of the Hermetic Tradition has been manifested in Ancient Egypt, another part in India and is committed to writing in e.g. Upanishads, yet another part in Tibet. And to this day, fragments of this knowledge are preserved, they differ from each other, but they speak of the same thing, for their source is one and the same. They are united by one common fundamental idea - man's reaching of man's Higher Self. But the paths and methods of reaching the Higher Self for a Tibetan will differ from those for a Hindu. At the same time, all the methods belong to the same Hermetic Tradition.

The School of Alchemy on the Argonauts' Ship has at its disposal the effective practices of the Hermetic Tradition which can help a disciple to reach his Higher Self.

Many people who try to study Sufism believe that only the Islamic tradition carries comprehensive knowledge, and this is their big mistake. Therefore, the Indian musician and spiritual Sufi Master Inayat Khan tried to breach this narrow understanding. Here are his words about comprehending the Almighty:

'I dare not think to raise my eyes to see Thy radiant image. I sit quietly by the lake of my heart, contemplating Thine reflection in it.'

Inayat Khan was an initiate of the tradition of the fire of the Parsu Belt, for his Teacher and initiator was from the Caucasus.

The word 'Sophia' is a part of the names of many spiritual movements, like e.g. 'Theosophy', and we too call our tradition 'Cosmosophy'. The Mother of God is the manifestation of Sophia, and the infant Jesus reminds us of the divine child, who is deep in us, in our essence.

The tradition of universal wisdom, Sophia, exists for many millions of years and is located not on our planet and not even in our Solar System, but in other solar systems, in other constellations. The disciple can join and study it only if he wants to reach his Higher Self.

This Tradition, which is also called 'stellar brotherhood' or 'higher humanity' consists for the most part of enlightened human beings. They are able to help us to advance along the Path of Enlightenment, but we need to be able to get in touch with them. For this the disciple needs:

• repeatedly going through the stage of purification, getting rid of heavy karma, through repentance and confession of mortal sins to the priest, reconsideration-exercise of the disciple's life and prayer of forgiveness;
• performing regularly the practice of awakening, that is Kriya Yoga.

The stellar brotherhood exists for millions of years on eighty-eight star systems of our Orion Ring, and the main constellation where this stellar knowledge is preserved and amassed is the constellation Orion.

Chapter 61. About the Path of Ascent which is built on the Mystical Ship. To contact the cosmic Tradition, you need to go through an alchemical transformation

The School has built a Path that unites the Hermetic and Christian traditions, following which you can obtain the Golden Fleece, that is alchemical, spiritual gold and achieve Enlightenment. The advancement on the Path of Ascent takes place through performing effective spiritual practices, which has been shared by the cosmic Tradition with the Earth. The goal of a disciple who has embarked on this Path and performs those practices is to reach his Higher Self and unite with the Creator of the Universe, to find Divine love in his heart.

The practices on the Path of Ascent include as follows:
Hermetic Tradition
1. Cleansing practice: The disciple's reconsideration of his horizontal life in order to get rid of the heavy karma of the past;
2. Practice of awakening: Kriya yoga in combination with prayer to the Lord or tuning in to universal spiritual Schools;
3. Practices of refining the coarse energy. Taoist practices of sublimation of instinctive and sexual energy;
4. Training under the guidance of the Master, who conveys the Ray of the stellar Tradition;
5. Acceptance of corrections from the Master and senior students;
6. Withstanding psychological pain when the disciple is admonished for his negative qualities;

The paragraphs 4, 5 and 6 have a collective name 'alchemical melting'. The disciple's ability to withstand deliberately alchemical melting makes it possible to dry out the damp, swampy spots of his soul, which are the habitat of all kinds of low, evil spirits, of our dark twin. Those spots are at the same time the disciple's sore points, as he feels resentment when admonitions of the Master or senior disciples hit his attachment to passions, to comfort; his unwillingness to perform the practices of cleansing and awakening, scepticism and all other negative qualities that darken the soul.

Christian tradition.
1. The disciple's confession of his sins to the priest;
2. Prayers of forgiveness to untie karmic knots with neighbours;
3. Confession for the whole life according to the confessional manuals;
4. Fostering virtues in oneself, performing works of mercy;
5. Learning to live according to the commandments of Christ.

Before contacting the cosmic Tradition, a neophyte must be hermetically prepared. The soul of a neophyte is as a rule raw, which means that it is mostly guided by impulses, instincts, sex and simple emotions. This means that it must be alchemically melted in order to separate the coarse from the subtle, or in simple terms, should be dried up. Alchemists call it transmutation of lead or of the ore into precious metals. The lead or the ore here signify a coarse soul, while precious metals and especially gold signify an enlightened soul which has found contact with the Creator of the Universe.

A person whose lead is transformed into gold is called the Master-alchemist.

Chapter 62. About the necessary conditions for the alchemical reaction. What does 'being placed in the alchemical crucible' mean

Indispensable conditions for the alchemical transformation of lead into gold:

1. The Secret, or Heavenly Fire. The Secret, or Heavenly Fire is the purest spiritual fire which only a Master-alchemist can receive from God. The Master thus has spiritual fire and divine knowledge at his disposal. The Master-alchemist is himself that very Philosopher's Stone, the Magisterium, as it is he who supplies the Heavenly Fire to melt the substances, he knows all the necessary ingredients, the degrees of the intensity of fire and the laws and regularities of the alchemical process. The alchemical process cannot be launched and go forth without the Master-alchemist, a disciple cannot transform his ore and lead on his own.

2. The Ore mixed with Natural Gold and Lead, that is a disciple. A disciple is a person who has set his heart on achieving unity with the Lord, in spite of any difficulties. The disciple in alchemy is the ore, mixed with natural gold (his positive qualities) and lead (his uroboros), from which spiritual, elevated gold must be smelted. The smelting occurs when the disciple's ore, natural gold and lead are placed in a hermetic crucible, which is then placed in the alchemical furnace, called Athanor and melted under various heating profiles for many years. Actually the process of alchemical transformation of a disciple can last during his entire incarnation. It might be accelerated only by the disciple's optional extra performing of practices of awakening and conscious suffering.

3. A tightly sealed alchemical Crucible is a set of rules of behaviour that a disciple should stick to for the correct process of the alchemical transformation of his soul.

These rules include:

- repeatedly going through the purification stage;
- performing the practice of awakening, Kriya Yoga;
- performing the Taoist practices for the transformation of instinctive and sexual energy;
- self-observation and relieving the tensions with other disciples;
- non-expression of negative emotions;
- readiness for conscious suffering;
- acceptance of corrections by the Master and senior disciples;
- withstanding the alchemical melting without throwing off the heightened mental temperature, which dries up the damp spots of the disciple's soul;
- reconsideration of undigested inner pain caused by alchemical melting;
- preservation of the substance of the meaning of life (that is sperm).

4. Right people, place and time means that the process of alchemical transformation requires a teaching situation in a place of heightened spiritual energy, in the presence of a Master of alchemy. During the melting, the disciple experiences psychological pain. The pain comes when a blow is struck at his pride and feeling of self-importance.

Chapter 63. How can you tell a real Master from a fake one? About the need to search for the Master. About the three types of influence: A, B and C. About the influence of the Sun and the Moon

The Hermetic tradition says that the Master is a person who has reached his Higher Self, that is he has completed the process of alchemical transformation and obtained inner gold.

And if the person has not completed his studying in the alchemical School, where his soul was transformed, he pretends to be a person who has inner gold. He begins to imitate the Master and this is called guru-business.

How can you tell a real Master from a fake one? Everyone is given absolute freedom in this matter. A person can make a mistake, but this is everyone's risk. Try to find a real Master using your magnetic centre.

Each person can develop on his own only to a certain level, then he must look for a Master, for his own achievements have a ceiling. And then help is needed from real Schools, and the person must try to find them.

There are three types of influences affecting a person living on Earth:

A - the influence of horizontal life. Every person experiences from the moment of his birth the influence of his environment, which determines his basic life attitudes. At the same time, a person's attention is often fixed on the illusory dream of maya, that is the common programs of the horizontal life: parental nursing, nursery school, secondary school, high school, work, family, giving birth to a child(ren). Then you need to launch your child(ren) into the same program, then wait until they give birth to their children and then you can pass away in peace. There is no room for spiritual development in a horizontal life. If a person falls out of the generally accepted framework, then he becomes a black sheep.

B – is the influence of culture, is the influence of literature, films, art in general, science, as well as religious institutions, and other spiritual organizations, accessible to everyone.

C – is the influence which comes from a spiritual Master, that is a person who has found contact with the Creator of the Universe and Divine love is in his heart. The Master establishes a School where he can share the Ray of Divine energies with his disciples and lead them through the transformational process in order to prepare them for the afterlife in the higher worlds. A disciple can develop the ability to perceive the subtle energy of the higher worlds by performing the practices of cleansing and awakening. Our raw, untransformed soul cannot endure Divine energies, a person can die or go crazy. It is like a real meeting with the astral fire, of which the body of an Angel consists. An unprepared soul can burn out in this fire.

In order to prepare his soul for contact with the higher worlds, a disciple should let the 'raw spots' of his soul, these are his 'sore points', horizontal attachments and passions, be alchemically 'dried up'. And this is achieved by performing spiritual practices and withstanding manly the fire of alchemical melting, that is accepting admonitions and correctional comments of the Master.

Chapter 64. About different levels of existence in the Universe. The vertical and horizontal scale of human values. About the earthly soul, the universal soul and the Higher Self. What does it mean to love a person

There are different levels of existence in the Universe. There is a material level inhabited by minerals, plants, animals and people. There is an astral level, where our astral bodies go after death. Each planet is surrounded by eight astral spheres. The fourth sphere is the purgatory, the first three spheres are hell, and life in the spheres above the purgatory is similar to life on earth, and what is called paradise. There live in those higher spheres the angels, too, the light beings who serve the Lord. They have a human-like body with huge wings. Each incarnated person has his own spiritual guardian angel until the age of twenty-eight.

Man can choose between the two possible scales of values:

1. The vertical scale of values:

Amongst God's creations man has the greatest value. The first priority is man's work on unfolding his spiritual abilities, his higher Self and uniting his essence in Divine love with the Creator of the Universe, and then this is the Path of Light.
Following this Path, a person gradually abandons egoistic attitudes and begins to sincerely take an interest in his neighbours, takes care of them, and inspires them to climb along the Holy Mountain. According to the universal law of analogy, the angels in heaven help such a person too and raise him to the higher worlds of Light.

2. Horizontal scale of values:

The main thing is power over people, money, comfort and other pleasures of life. This is an infernal approach and it leads into darkness.

It is important to understand what is the difference between body, soul and essence. The physical body is a kind of temporary space suit necessary for life in the material world. The soul longs for outer impressions and emotions, therefore it very often loses itself in a multitude of earthly temptations. Only our essence can climb up to the higher worlds and meet our Father in Heaven.

Earthly love means possessing a person's body, indulging his habits and feeling his warmth. This has nothing to do with the Path of Light. To love a person means to love not only his physical body or soul, but to help him to find and manifest his higher origin and to reach his higher Self.

However in order to be capable of loving a person that deeply, the disciple needs to be a real (lady)knight, a kind of Don Quixote, who is always ready to support and inspire his comrades on the Path of Enlightenment.

Many people have experienced the cruelty and injustice of the world and the hostility of the Universe towards human beings. Indeed, if a person, without going through the stage of purification, tries to meditate and contact the higher worlds, he might be captured by demons which pretend to be angels of light, deceiving the inexperienced seeker, whose consciousness has not been purified.

Chapter 65. Formation of the magnetic centre: spiritual quest. In search of the alchemical School and the Master. Harmonization of the magnetic centre

When man becomes interested in Ancient Egypt, Buddhism, Christianity and other spiritual doctrines, when his soul begins to collect heavenly jewels bit by bit, a magnetic centre gradually begins to form inside him. This new organ helps man in his search for spiritual path. This is the first step towards awakening the essence of man - the spark of the Great Absolute. For the essence, unity with the Heavenly Father is the most natural desire.

However during his search man begins to feel helpless after a while, because the things he is looking for do not exist in ordinary life.

He begins then to look for the spiritual Schools, for the spiritual Masters who can show him the Path to heaven.

And if a person finds an esoteric School that is really linked to heaven, and if he will not miss the chance that the School offers, then he is very lucky. And if he manages to meet the stellar Tradition, huge opportunities will open before him, which before he could not even suspect. If the magnetic centre has been incorrectly developed, it must be harmonized. Having got on the Ship of the Argonauts, the disciple absorbs the knowledge of the stellar Tradition and, performing the practices of awakening, advances along the Path of Enlightenment.

14th November 1993, The Hague, lecture

The Hermetic Tradition became active in Russia sometime in 1920, in the difficult times that followed the Russian revolution. At that time it was deeply hidden, otherwise it would have been destroyed. And now it begins to manifest itself in Holland, it becomes accessible.

We must realize that this unique School, representing a stellar tradition, really exists here and now. Only then will we be able to fully participate in it.

The 20th century is a very interesting period from a cosmic point of view. It began in 1914 when World War I broke out in Europe. People are used to thinking that everything that happens to them happens only to them. In fact, major events take place in other parts of the universe. The war that brought with it so much change, suffering and pain to Europe, was a reflection of the major battle which took place in the remote astral world. And then, a helping hand from above, which is always given by the spiritual powers of light, was extended. And then many souls were incarnated which were capable of rendering this aid. In Russia, which was in a particularly difficult situation, there were especially many of them: G. Gurdjieff, P. Ouspensky and many other known and unknown people. This age is very materialistic, and therefore they have made efforts in order to share the new impulse with those who were able to accept it. It is impossible to share it with all of humanity, but only with those whose souls woke up from horizontal sleep and aspired towards heaven.

Chapter 66. On how a disciple can convey the current of light. What happens to a disciple who has fallen under the influence of dark forces. How to get out of negative states. It is important to understand what state you are in

2ᵈ December 1993, The Hague, van Speijkstraat, questions answered

1. Master G: 'Negative emotions do belong to a person, but when he gains personal power, he begins to convey through himself certain winds, especially in a dense astral atmosphere. If he gives free rein to his mechanical manifestations, then he is no more alert in situations, and can become very quickly a tributary of the dark current, conveying cold energy that shuts off the spiritual heart.

2. If a disciple regularly purifies his soul and alchemically transforms his coarse composition, he obtains gradually the so called 'positive crystallization' which keeps him on the path of Light. For it is important, interesting and pleasant for him to share with the world the ideas of the Path of Enlightenment, subtle vibrations of the higher worlds, ideas and ideals of the knighthood of light. However this is valid only for the evolved disciples, who appreciate keenly the atmosphere of the Master and the alchemical Ray. As a rule, such disciples suffered a lot in the past, cleansed their souls from sins and passions and obtained the qualities of mercy, compassion and love. The sensitivity of the disciple's spiritual heart is always determined by the history of his soul, his achievements in past incarnations. Thus, a disciple who practiced Kriya yoga retains his spiritual achievements with regard to the transformation of his consciousness and subtle bodies in the following incarna-

tions. This is the key to his rapid progress along the Path of Enlightenment.

3. Horizontal people are capable of conveying only the chaos and confusion of worldly life through themselves. If a person is heavily burdened with karma, then he is unable to distinguish light from darkness. He perceives dark vibrations, gets a luciferic kick from this and begins to invisibly manipulate people around. Then the demons use him as a puppet to destroy his soul forever. In such a person, a dark double grows strongly, which is a hotbed of passions and vices. Many people, who just got in touch with cold energy, begin to consider themselves important and significant people. Kasyan, for example, after his six-month stay in the City of Fools in the company of local mafiosi, came back transformed into a real rogue. He got a kind of paranoia and thought that everyone who could harm or betray him should be eliminated. He went to the City of Fools to undergo a test on his Path, with an idea to work on the city and to improve its atmosphere. However it turned out just the other way around, the city worked on him and infected him with its dark ideas and attitudes.

You, Kasyan, need to start chasing not only the dark states, but also the light ones. But first, cleanse your soul through repentance and reconsideration of your grievances, of which you have amassed a lot. Instead, you threaten your insulters with reprisals; punish those who hurt your inflated pride, actually, those, who tried to stop your dragon. In order not to sink into darkness completely, you need to track your negative chaotic 'selves' and make their portraits. And when they would become active, you can recognize the enemy by sight and bring them to justice, that is let the Heavenly Fire of the Ray incinerate them during a next in turn alchemical melting. Thus the dark part of your soul will have less room and you will have less false attitudes. It is also important to observe your working 'selves' and to describe your elevated states in your diary so that these notes can inspire you to go on with spiritual work. Being in a negative state, you can always open your diary and plunge into the light you've felt before. The Argonaut needs to gain experience of a quick abandoning of his negative states by learning to switch attention to the spiritual side of being, for example, by praying to the Lord Jesus Christ, or performing Kriya Yoga with concentration in the centre of the chest, where our essence abides. It is necessary to chase for our elevated states, for they awaken the essence. If you work hard on yourself, undergoing the alchemical transformation, cleansing the spiritual heart from the packed up horizontal soot, then after a while you can feel the grace emanating from the Creator of the Universe.

Kasyan sometimes gets high on certain kinds of astral emanations, neglecting self-observation. It seems to him that he still belongs to the current of light, while staying in the City of Fools he switched to the current of mafia, a current of darkness and now insults people, crushes them as if they are ants. However this is not his own power, but a dark mediumistic influx.

Remember that the disciple can convey through himself the current of light as well as the current of darkness. It is important to distinguish between them. So, the dark current manifests itself through the disciple's excessive pride, lack of consideration for the interests of others, resentment, anger, aggression, cold heart. In an elevated state, on the contrary, the disciple wants to share heartfelt warmth and joy with his neighbours, take care of them, because he becomes truly interested in them, spiritual fire kindles in his heart, and serene love and grace reign in his soul.

Chapter 67. Having become crystallized, we act mechanically. Discussion on building the School space

2^d December 1993 The Hague, Van Speijkstraat, evening, after the workshop, conversation

Master G: 'On the Ship of Fools, we learn how to become 'amateurs' again, we learn to unlearn, because crystallization has occurred in us, and we do everything automatically. For we have become professionals, and now we act and work mechanically, through our 'knaves', as Burton would say. We are too much identified with our associations and cannot accept anything new, we do not feel a new impulse. We are afraid to make mistakes, but mistakes are the most wonderful thing, because we learn from them.
……
Women are much stronger linked to their family tree than men and carry out biological reproduction programs through themselves. They stick more often to group consciousness and convey the all-women wind, while men are inclined to stick to their individual consciousness. During the building of the School Centre, we tried to protect this place from both Dutch and Russian women, so that they would not bring their own chaos there and/or establish their own rules. But now, when we managed to establish our lines of power here, women are allowed too, of course. However now they will no longer be able to re-magnetize the atmosphere we've created here. Remember how Durva distorted the whole situation in Dodrecht, and she managed to re-magnetize her husband with her programs. As a result the Centre for studying of Arcana in his house collapsed.
'What can a woman do in the School space then?' Annika asked.

'You were specially invited to live here so that you would understand what the School is.' answered G. 'This is exactly the place where your soul can develop.'

'Where there is a possibility to perform practices of awakening,' added Kasyan. 'It was not possible to build the School atmosphere in Satya's house in Dodrecht, because you, Annika, forced it out and established your own, female rules. Irina came from Moscow, just like you with a complete lack of understanding of what the School is and with a subconscious desire to destroy any subtle situation.' 'The one who owns the place establishes his or her rules there,' G added, 'if a woman is the owner of the territory, then she dictates her own rules of life and existence. It is difficult to build a solid house, but no one realizes how much more difficult it is to build a vertical atmosphere and to establish the lines of power in the right way. This requires much more effort, and even more efforts are required to preserve the vertical atmosphere, to protect it from various chaotic attacks of the environment. It is difficult for Annika to understand this, for she has no experience, but Satya studied at many seminars at the Osho Centre and knows how difficult it is to build an ashram. But, if you, Annika, develop spiritually and grow, then you can become an assistant in building the ashram and protect it, protect the School's atmosphere.'

'The desire of a woman to destroy the vertical life of a man,' Annika said, 'seems absolutely appropriate from the point of view of nature.'

'The important thing is what you choose yourself,' said Satya, 'the vertical or the horizontal?'

'And you need to make this choice every day,' Master G added, 'because a person often forgets to do what he has planned. And we wanted to create a women's lodge precisely so that a woman would learn to contribute to the vertical striving of a man, to help him, and not to castrate him spiritually.

The women's lodge is not meant for struggle against men, but to create a harmonious coexistence with men. That is to create a spiritual atmosphere, not a women's zoo. Men have so many problems because in everyday life women as a rule know better how to live as is the convention. If a man does something wrong from her point of view, he immediately is qualified as a scoundrel, all the cliches are hung on him, because a woman always knows best. However she is mostly a conveyer of horizontal programs and this is her strength for a woman is strongly supported by nature, and at the same time her weakness, when it goes about the vertical dimension.

On the Ship, a woman should not demand constant attention and care from a man. If she cannot help, then at least let her not interfere.

A woman needs to get rid of her claims and consumer attitudes towards man.

She needs to realize that it is better to use the time and opportunity of her incarnation with dignity, that is to struggle for the freedom of her essence, rather than to chase after the short-term earthly happiness.

Chapter 68. About the spiritual patronage of St. Nicholas the Wonderworker and the holy apostles John the Theologian, Peter and Andrew the First-Called. About Martha and Mary

5th December 1993, The Hague, Borelstraat. Master G's answer to the question: 'What to do?'

Santa Claus is Saint Nicholas the Wonderworker and God's pleaser, who patronizes all pilgrims. He alone is responsible for the entire Earth, in one hand he holds the Temple of God, in the other - a sword. New Year is not a simple holiday, but a mystery, one of the most powerful mysteries in the entire cosmos. No wonder we see the word 'Nika' on the cross. Nika is the goddess of Victory, there is a connection with the name Nikolai, the victory over the powers of darkness.

The Gospel says: 'And the light shines in the darkness, and the darkness did not comprehend it.' (John 1, 5). The first fourteen lines of the Gospel of John are a gateway to the unknown dimension of ancient Rosicrucianism. Through this it is possible to penetrate into the world of the holy Apostle John, who spread his wings over Russia. The supreme apostle Peter spread his wings over Western Europe, but he did it on the level of Martha, and John - on the level of Mary. And through wanderings and pilgrimages, through travels on the Ship of Fools, you can join this. The Ship carries many secrets, although it looks so nondescript. However it is only the Ship that can bring you to the faraway kingdom. But at any moment it can abandon an unprepared sailor. The 16th Arcanum card depicts a tower with the lord of the earthly kingdom falling down along one side of it, and with the lord of the spiritual hierarchy falling down along the other side of it, because they do not know the central teaching, the inner core. To pass this

Arcanum, you need to strengthen your horizontal and vertical being.

There is another apostle - Saint Andrew the First-Called, the founder of the Byzantine church, who was crucified on a dynamic cross. It is a rotating cross and a rotating self-sacrifice, when you sacrifice even what you do not possess. And sacrifice opens access to cosmic life. This is already the theme of the XIIth Arcanum, which a disciple who has embarked on the Path of Enlightenment has to deal with throughout his life.

You must know by heart Borges' short story 'Aleph'. It relates how a person from a mere nobody turns into the king of cosmic consciousness. In the Bhagavad Gita, Krishna wanted to show Arjuna a hole in his sock, but showed billions of galaxies in an instance of time instead. And then Krishna began to rely on the humility of his disciple. And the horizontal is always proud of itself and it has monopoly on the truth which for the horizontal is making money, procreation, creating a good family. But all this good family will still one day lie in a coffin.

And the West has been dissociated from the real spiritual life and what we are trying to do now is to breathe a new spark into the life of Western Europe. At the level of pancakes, Western Europe is good, but this is the level of Martha, who baked pancakes and presented them to Christ, and He said to her: 'Martha, Martha, you are anxious and troubled over many things. And yet only one thing is necessary.' (Luke 10:41,42) But Mary chose something else, 'the best portion' (John 10:42). She did not bother about pancakes, she was so focused on Christ's words that she did not even serve pancakes to Him, as she was concerned about something else, about heavenly things.

Likewise, disciples following the Path of Enlightenment need to strive with all their hearts towards the Heavenly Father.

Let us recall a wonderful aphorism: 'We must live our way, that is the honest way.'

After all, the prayer says not 'My Father', but 'Our Father', that is, we have a common egregorial task to be completed. When the vertical conscience awakens in you, you will immediately understand what you need to do. For it is useless for you to give advice now, you anyway will transform this advice inside you in something completely different. And when your vertical conscience awakens, and you will live our way, the honest way, all your questions will disappear immediately.

A warrior cannot be given advice on how to fight. If you live only by horizontal values and desires, you are in the deep rear, which is a wretched existence. But you can choose for taking risks and dealing with flying bullets by going to the front line that is to perform the practices of awakening, cleanse your soul by repentance, cultivate virtues, perform works of mercy, and follow the commandments of Jesus Christ.'

Chapter 69. The School helps disciples to immerse in themselves. About the relationship between the Master and the disciple. About three types of disciples in the fairy tales

Master G said: 'We need to understand that we must form together a fairly stable group, the members of which are trying to immerse in themselves and find a link to the Lord. And then, all lectures and practical exercises will fall on fertile ground.

We must become the core, and then it doesn't matter whether new people come or not, because they will fall into the atmosphere that we will build together. But only together can we build this atmosphere in order to go deeper inside ourselves. And most importantly, so that we can learn to be friends and be sincere with each other, communicate at the level of the heart. And we must all understand that we are all together the School. And all together we can create a cup for the perception of new knowledge, that vessel in which the transformation of the soul of each of us can take place. And we will gradually begin to change, and the circumstances of life will begin to change together with us.'

One of the disciples, Elise, remarked: 'I got a glimpse of the significance of what is happening now!'

Her friend Sufiya added: 'My capabilities and abilities increase in the atmosphere of this place, and now I can do even those difficult things that I could not do before.'

'Let us now try to consider the question of the relationship between the Master and the disciple in the School,' continued G. 'The Master has to work upon all the centres of the disciple. If he works only upon his head, that is only to give lectures and explain, the Argonaut will only have information about the School, but he will not have any experiences. If the Master would work only upon the disciple's emotions, without elucidations, the disciple will have only very vague memories of what happened, for people very quickly forget their emotional states. Therefore, the Master works simultaneously upon all the centres, the intellectual, emotional and instinctive-motoric ones, as well as on the disciple's ear and speech apparatus, because many things are transmitted through intonation, and not through the content of words. All chakras of the disciple must participate in the obtaining of knowledge. To do this, the disciple needs to pass repeatedly the Albedo stage and withstand alchemical melting.

A person can be compared to a house: the upper floor is the upper chakras of a person, the middle floor is the emotional centre, and the basements, the foundation on which the whole house rests, is the instinctive-motoric centre. Therefore, if you build a house on a deficient foundation, it will soon collapse.

Remember the tale of the three little pigs. To survive the winter and protect themselves from the wolf, each piglet had built a house for itself. One piglet had built his house of straw, the second one had built his house of wood and twigs, the third one had built his house of stone. Just three times the wolf blew on the first house, and it flew into the wind, just five times the wolf blew on the second house and it collapsed, but no matter how many times the wolf blew on the third house, it still stood firmly and securely. The wolf in this tale is a symbol of the influences of external life. Similar to the three piglets, there are three types of disciples. The first work only upon their intellectual centre, the second understand that it is necessary to work upon their emotional centre as well. But life quickly destroys the precarious constructions of those disciples. The third type of disciples work on all their inner centres with the help of the practices of awakening. This is the guarantee of their inner stability and allows them to overcome the obstacles that arise on the Path of Enlightenment.

In another tale, of the goldfish, the disciples of the first and second types are symbolized by a greedy and wayward old woman. Such disciples only want to consume large amounts of information and have different experiences. Just like the old woman wanted first a new trough, then a new house, then she wanted to become a lady, then a queen, and then she wanted to have the goldfish at her complete disposal after which the goldfish took back all her gifts and the old woman again had nothing but her broken old trough. In the tale, the goldfish symbolize the alchemical School.'

There are plenty of opportunities for spiritual development on the Ship of Fools, but it is important not to seize the merits of the cosmic Ray and continue working hard on yourself, passing all the stages of alchemical transformation.

So that was a mosaic-like answer to your question 'What to do?'.

Supplement: Practices of Purification and Awakening

Quotations from Konstantin Serebrov's autobiography entitled 'Spiritual Breath. The Practice of Kriya Yoga'

Prayer of forgiveness., p.68

'Kasyan went to church every day and used the lists that he had made for reconsideration to recall his sins and he confessed them, one by one, every day, to the priest. 'You are a proud man,' the priest said to Kasyan's after his turn to confess. 'You extol yourself in front of other people and therefore you condemn them. God does not appreciate the proud, and He does not come to you. And you are suffering because God's love is not in you.' On another occasion the priest said to Kasyan: 'Learn to forgive other people and God will also forgive you your sins.' Kasyan prayed to the Mother of God to rid him from his jealousy of Irina, an old love of his. They had broken long ago, but Kasyan still felt the break like an open wound and could not forget all the angry, horrible words they had said to each other, and even worse were their negative feelings towards each other, a mixture of hatred and fatal attraction that hurt him the most. Suddenly, as he stood gazing at the icon, a prayer came into his head, as a gift from above. 'O most holy Mother of God, as I stand before you I ask Irina to forgive me all my insults that I caused by word, deed and thought; known and unknown to me.

O most holy Mother of God, standing before you, I forgive Irina all her insults to me that she caused by word, deed and thought, known and unknown to me.

Let me not condemn her, but let God judge me.' Immediately after this prayer Kasyan felt that his soul had become lighter, as if part of the black deposits deep inside had evaporated by the invisible fire of his prayer. 'On one hand, my soul is purified by confession,' Kasyan though with a warm feeling of joy in his heart. 'On the other hand, now I can perform this myself, with the help of the Mother of God. Now the whole process will go much quicker...'

The Kriya technique, p. 42

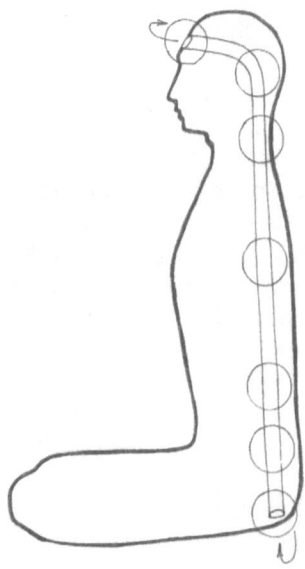

Illustration 4. Circulation of energy during Kriya breathing

Sit down in the half-lotus posture,' Alexey continued, 'or on a chair, with an upright back. Watch your spine constantly as it has the tendency to bend forward.
You should not lean your back towards any object as your energy will flow away. In order for you to have a good idea of the sensations during this practice, carry out the fol-

lowing procedures: place the edge of your left palm with half-bended fingers on the upper edge of the right hand so that they form a kind of tube. Inhale air through this tube, pronouncing a long sound 'O-o-o-u-u-u' - the air will feel cool. Breathe the air out then, right above the fingers, pronouncing the sound 'I-i-i' at the same time, the air will now feel warm. Both sounds should come from the depth of the throat. Repeat this ten times in order to remember the sensation.

Put your hands together on your knees. Imagine that your spine is a kind of empty tube: one end is the coccyx and the other the third eye. Breathe in, moving at the same time your life energy, your prana, inside the 'tube' from coccyx to the third eye, while pronouncing the sound 'O-OU'.

Still breathing in, move your prana forward through the bridge of the nose to the point a distance of a couple of centimetres in front of the bridge of your nose, and then bring it back, making a U-turn and moving your prana through the point right above the third eye, back into your head. Breathing out, move your prana downwards along the rear of the 'tube' of your spine, back to the coccyx while pronouncing the sound 'I' at the same time. The inhalation is accompanied by a sensation of coolness inside the spinal 'tube', while the exhalation is accompanied by a sensation of warmth along the rear of the spinal 'tube'. The cool energy has a light blue colour, while the warm energy has a rosy colour. The inhalations and exhalations last 10-15 seconds; thus one cycle of Kriya breath lasts 20-30 seconds.

At the beginning you can exercise for half an hour in the morning and in the evening, which is equal to 120 Kriya breaths a day.'

'What makes prana move up and down along the spine? Is it just breathing?' asked Kasyan.

'The driving force is our will power,' answered Alexey, 'and breathing also helps in this respect. Normally our life energy, that is prana, circulates around our nervous system and maintains the activity of our organism. The moving

prana makes our spine a kind of magnet, which draws all our life energy from the muscles, the inner organs and the five senses. When this happens we are not aware of the outer world, but come into a state of spiritual contemplation. In such a state our prayer to Lord God becomes ten times more effective.
A joyful, cool and refreshing sensation on the entire trajectory from the coccyx to the third eye during inhalation, is a sign that you are performing the 'spiritual breath', as I call it, in a correct way.'

Inhalation and exhalation combined with the lifting and lowering of energy, can be carried out with a prayer instead of sounds. You may use a short prayer: 'Lord Jesus Christ (while inhaling), have mercy on me (while exhaling)', or the full prayer 'Lord Jesus Christ (while inhaling), have mercy on me, the sinner (while exhaling)'. You may plead for purification or for illumination too, or pray to the Mother of God. See for more prayers the above mentioned book.

Quotations from Konstantin Serebrov's 'Pray and Work (on Yourself)'

Exercise to regain the Energy of the Soul which was lost in the Past., p. 53

...By using an exercise which is a combination of the exercises of the Kriya and Tao monks, and of the Toltec magicians, you can work on purifying your soul.
'It must be impossible to combine the exercises from such different traditions!' Michael exclaimed.
'These exercises belong to the ancient integral hermetic tradition and they have the same purpose: to purify and to spiritualise your energy. Therefore, their combination is not only effective, but even more effective than each of them separately.

It is better to do the exercise early in the morning. Sit down on a chair which is covered with a woollen blanket, with crossed shinbones, to shortcut the nerve channels. The left shinbone should be placed before the right one.

Recall and keep in your memory your acquaintances from the past, in communication with whom you have lost much of your soul's energy.

1. While inhaling, pull in through the point (E) on your belly, which is located two fingers below the navel, the energy of your soul which has been spent in the past, and move it to your backbone and further along the nerve column to the point between the eyebrows. The nerve cord rises from the base of the coccyx to medulla oblongata in the back of the head. The nerve cord has a width of about 14 mm in women and 20 mm in men.

While inhaling, turn your head slightly to the left; at the same time pull the energy into your spine and raise it along the nerve cord and then along the middle line of your head right into point C between your eyebrows.

2. While exhaling, move the energy of the soul along a curve around the point (C) back into your head, and further along the nerve channels inside your head and the outer side of the 'pipe' of your spine to point (A) in your crotch. After that, move it along the nerve channel of the middle line of your lower belly, and allow it to flow into the hollow sphere (F) which is the size of a tennis ball and is located in the centre of the lower part of your belly. While performing the above-mentioned you should exhale slowly so that at this point you have exhaled just half of the air from your lungs.

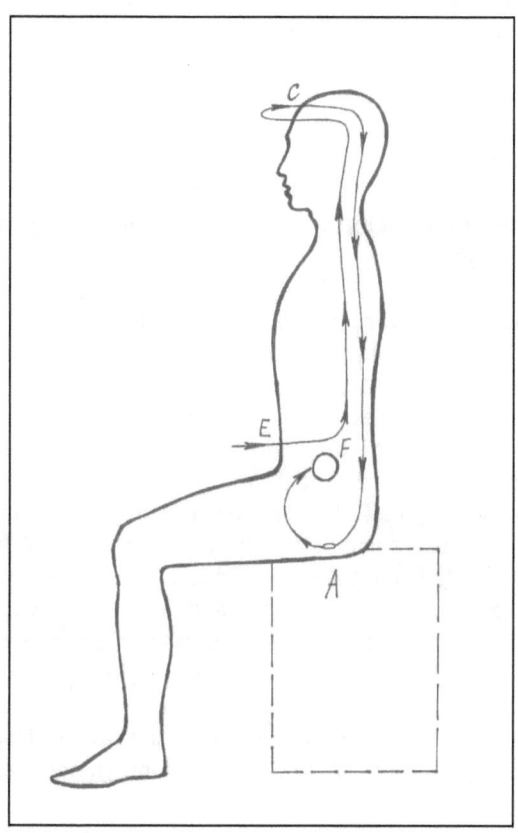

Illustration 1. Regaining the Energy of the Soul

3. Hold your breath and move your head rhythmically from left to right and back for about 5-7 seconds. Then, after opening your larynx and letting the air out of your lungs, keep on rotating your head rhythmically until you have exhaled fully.

Together with that air you should push out the energy of the person in question, which is heavy as a rule. By moving your head, you break your mental and physical bond with the past and get back the lost energy and power of the soul.

You, Michael, must perform this exercise for at least two hours every day; otherwise you will not be able to get rid of your profane past.
'And what if I only have pleasant memories of my past,' asked Michael, 'why should I erase them, how possibly could they disturb me...'

A simplified Technique to restore the Energy of the Soul, p. 69

'While inhaling, turn your head to the left. At the same time breathe in the energy of the soul that you have lost in a particular situation, through the point on your belly which is located two fingers below the navel.
Turn your head to the right, breathing out the remembrances of your sinful acts through the nose. Breathe out approximately half of the air from your lungs. Hold your breath for five seconds and rock your head slightly and rhythmically from right to left, and back several times. In this way you break your ethereal ties with that particular situation in your past. Then you must open your larynx and still rocking your head slightly, let the rest of the air escape from your lungs. At the same time, you should push out your heavy energy, together with the air. This lasts five seconds too. Then breathe in again and the entire cycle should be repeated.'

Exercises which help to overcome the Passion of Fornication, p. 109

There is another universal method, next to eating little food, which is no less effective in helping to curb the passion of fornication and other passions, such as anger, irritation and so on.' Kasyan continued. 'The human body lives by the energy which it takes from food. If this energy flows downwards, towards the instinctive area and further to the genitals, lustful designs emerge immediately. If this energy is directed upwards, then it is possible to open the heart. When the ascetic prays, energy taken from nutrition rises upwards, and his inner man, that is the soul, revives. As soon as he ceases to pray, the inner man dies, and only the external person, that is our body, lives. Energy falls into the area of instinct, and lustful designs start to invade the ascetic. In order to prevent this, it is necessary to begin at such moments an urgent sublimation of the sexual energy. When instinctive and sexual energy is moved upwards, lustful designs cease to invade the ascetic.'

'Well,' Michael remarked, 'when my Polly is just in the room where I am, I become obsessed with sexual desire'

'It is exactly the case,' continued Kasyan, 'when you have to perform an exercise called fast breathing:'

1. Sit with a straightened back, concentrate on your sexual centre or on your sexual desire. Then with the help of fast breathing: a speed of 50 breaths per minute, rotate sexual energy around the circular orbit of the neural channels, part of which is the spine (Ill. 2). The orbit begins in perineum (point A), then passes through the nervous channel of the spine, up to the crown (point B) and continues down the nervous channel, which passes along the front part of the body back to point A. Thus, with the help of such fast breathing, sexual energy is driven into the spine.

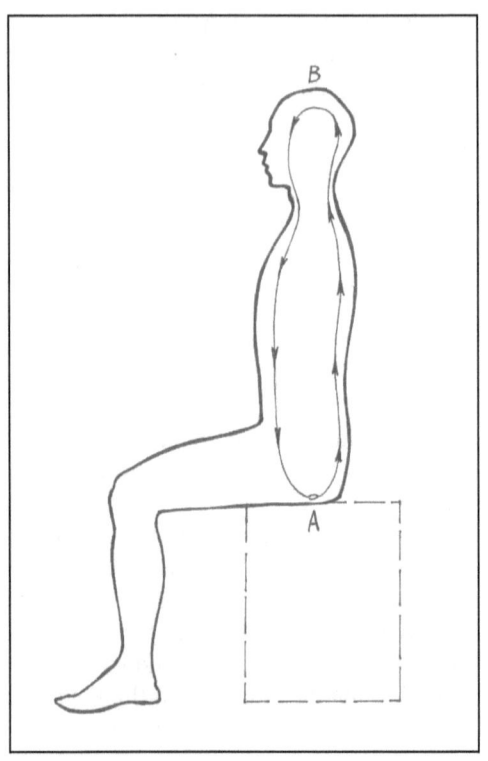

Illustration 2. The circular orbit. Fast Breathing

2. As soon as you feel that the spine is filled up with energy, move the energy into the area (F) that is situated in the centre of the bottom part of the abdomen (Ill. 3). For this purpose it is necessary to carry out the following. Feel, how while you inhale, energy rises from the coccyx along the nervous channel of the backbone to the point between the eyebrows. Then while you exhale the energy passes down the nervous channel, then along the front part of the body to the point situated approximately at the width of two fingers below the navel, and is driven into the round cavity (F), located in the centre of the lower part of the ab-

domen. The cavity is about the size of a tennis ball. Repeat the lifting and lowering of energy through the nervous channels, until all energy is transferred in this way from the backbone to the cavity (F) in the lower part of the abdomen.

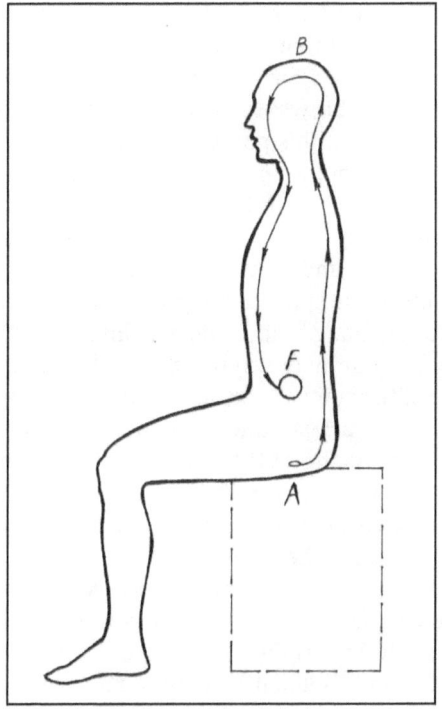

Illustration 3. Moving Energy into the Cavity in the Abdomen

3. As soon as you feel that the cavity (F) is filled with energy, then it is necessary to sublimate it and to bring it up to the centre of the head, in order to satiate your brain with it. For this purpose you need to hold your breath, then to make 9 circular rotations with the eyes counter clockwise.

Breathe out, and repeat this cycle of rotation three more times, which makes 36 rotations in total. When rotating, the eyes make a full circle, remaining open all the time. Then inhale again and while holding the breath make 6 circular rotations with the eyes clockwise. Repeat this cycle of rotation three times more, which will make 24 rotations. At this moment you will feel that the sexual energy has risen into the brain.

4. Then concentrate for several minutes on the point (C) between the eyebrows, so that the sublimed energy will be concentrated at this point. Further, to transfer this energy to the area of the spiritual heart, which is situated in the centre of the chest, it is necessary to draw this energy in while inhaling through point (E), situated two fingers below the navel, and to lift it with a breath, up the nervous channel of the spine to the point (C) between the eyebrows, still inhaling. And while exhaling move the energy down to the point between the shoulder blades, along the back side of the spinal 'tube', and from there bring it to the area of the heart (D) in the centre of the chest (Ill. 4). Repeat this until the heart feels filled up with warmth. Inhalation and exhalation, the lifting and lowering of energy, should be carried out with a prayer. You may use the most simple: 'Lord, have mercy on me'.

'After you have carried out this exercise correctly, your soul will quieten, and lustful desires and thoughts will cease to obsess you. This is the principal, universal exercise for purification and sublimation of all sorts of energies of the body and soul.

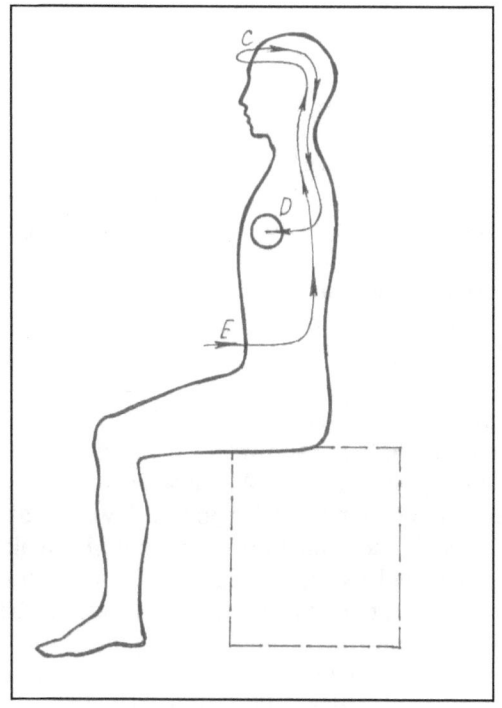

Illustratie 4. Storing of sublimated Energy in the Area of the Heart

It is better for you to carry out this exercise daily, twice a day: in the morning and in the evening. Then it will be easier for you to curb your flesh and establish a quieter relationship with Polina, so that you can follow the Path.'

The advanced Method to regain Energy of the Soul lost in the Past, p.119

'...Well, listen then,' Brother Kasyan said.
'For the recovery of lost psychical strength we use the same universal method of cleansing breathing, only with small variations. As in the simpler variant you have to sit comfortably on a chair without a back, and straighten the spine.

We must imagine our sexual partner, including the sensations we had. On inhaling through the point (E) (Ill. 1) which is two fingers below the navel, we draw in the lost energy from the past and bring it up the nervous channel of the spine to the point (C), which is situated right in the middle between the eyebrows. At the same time we turn our head slightly to the left. With a half exhalation we turn the head to the right and bring energy down the back side of the 'tube' of the spine to the perineum. Then along the nervous channel through the perineum gently up to the cavity (F). It is situated in the lower part of the abdomen, where the energy can be kept for a long time.

2. Then, while holding our breath for about five seconds, we slightly and rhythmically turn our head from right to left, breaking the energy ties with this woman. It is necessary to repeat this cycle until you feel a vibration in the area (F) in the bottom part of the abdomen.

3. Then it is necessary to start the sublimation of the retrieved psychic energy; for this purpose you have to bring it up and then saturate your brain with it. You should inhale, hold the breath and make nine circular rotations with your eyes counter clockwise and then exhale. Repeat this three more times; in total 36 rotations counter clockwise. While rotating, the eyes make a full circle, remaining open all the time.

Then take another breath, and while holding the breath make six circular rotations with the eyes in reverse direction, that is, clockwise, and then exhale. Repeat this three more times: in total 24 rotations clockwise. Thus you will feel, as the sexual energy has become sublimated in this way, that it has risen to the brain.

4. Then for five minutes concentrate on the point between the eyebrows, so that sublimated energy is focused at this point.

5. Furthermore, it is necessary to transfer this energy to the area (D) of the spiritual heart, which is situated in the centre of the chest (Ill. 4). For this it is necessary to do the following exercise: together with the breath bring the energy through the point (E) along the nervous channel of the spine up to the point (C) between the eyebrows. Then together with an exhalation bring it down to the point between the shoulder blades, along the backside of the 'tube' of the spine, and from there to the area of the heart (D) in the centre of the chest. Repeat this action until the heart fills with warmth. Inhalations and exhalations, the raising and lowering of energy, should be carried out with a prayer. You may say the simplest prayer: 'Lord, have mercy on me'.

At the end of this exercise you must put the sublimed energy into storage! For this purpose it is necessary to concentrate for five minutes on the cavity (F), meant for the storage of energy, in the abdomen below the navel (Ill. 1). You should feel how the energy rumble there, making this cavity vibrate.

If the sublimed energy is not stored, it is quickly wasted and will flow over to other people.'

'You are teaching him this practice in vain,' Brother Gouri remarked, 'he will never gather energy because he constantly makes love to Polina.'

'It is necessary to do all the exercises,' continued Kasyan, 'mentioned above: that is the retrieving of lost sexual energy, purification and its sublimation with the help of the rotation of the eyes, right after you have retrieved energy, without any breaks, one by one.

After the correct performance of these exercises you will feel a calmness in your soul, and sexual desires and lascivious thoughts will cease to obsess you.
It is recommended to carry out these exercises every day in the morning and in the evening.'

www.ingramcontent.com/pod-product-compliance
Lightning Source LLC
LaVergne TN
LVHW041709070526
838199LV00045B/1277